Vocabulary

EXPRESS
REVIEW GUIDES

Vocabulary

LEARNINGEXPRESS ®

OCM80460285

New York

Library of Congress Cataloging-in-Publication Data:
Express review guides. Vocabulary.—1st ed.
   p. cm.
   ISBN: 978-1-57685-628-4
   1. Vocabulary—Study and teaching (Secondary) 2. Vocabulary—Study and teaching (Middle school) I. LearningExpress (Organization)
   LB1631.E97 2007
428.1071'2—dc22

                                    2007001975

Printed in the United States of America

9   8   7   6   5   4   3   2   1

First Edition

ISBN: 978-1-57685-628-4

For more information or to place an order, contact LearningExpress at:
   55 Broadway
   8th Floor
   New York, NY 10006

Or visit us at:
   www.learnatest.com

Contents

Introduction
Vocabulary Is for Babies

Sticks and stones
May break my bones
But words will never hurt me.

We have all heard this playground chant before. Although it's a nice thought, the reason why this chant has been repeated by children for hundreds of years is because *it's not true*. Anyone who has ever been called a name before will confirm that words *can* hurt, often times much more than sticks and stones.

The English novelist Edward Bulwer-Lytton coined another famous phrase that you may have heard: *The pen is mightier than the sword*. By this, Bulwer-Lytton meant that a well-written argument can change the world more easily than violence.

As Bulwer-Lytton and the schoolyard chant recognize, words have a lot of power. Words are the basis of communication. Even babies recognize the importance of words. The first words babies speak are for the things that are most important to them, such as *mama*, *dada*, or *milk*. As babies grow and get older, they learn to use the right words in the right combinations to get the things they need and to learn more about the world around them.

That's great, you might think, but I'm not a baby. If you want to get a glass of milk, assuming you are *not* a baby, you can just go to the refrigerator and get one. So why should you care about learning vocabulary?

The answer is this: Learning the skills to understand new vocabulary words can help you, not just in school, but in life. As Bulwer-Lytton knew, being able to write and speak well is a valuable skill to have. People will listen to your opinions and enjoy reading your writing if you have a good vocabulary. This book will teach you not only the rules you need to succeed on vocabulary tests, but also the rules that will help you communicate effectively.

There is much more to learning new vocabulary words than just mere memorization. In many ways, words are like puzzles. If you learn the right strategies, you can often determine the meanings of words without looking at a dictionary.

For an example, take a look at the previous sentence:

> "If you learn the right strategies, you can often determine the meanings of words without looking at a dictionary."

When you read the word *dictionary*, you know immediately what it means. But what if you had never seen the word before? What strategies could you use to determine its meaning?

The first trick you might use is to think about other words that look similar. For *dictionary*, you might think of the words *diction* or *dictate*. Both of those words have something to do with language, so you can guess that a dictionary will have something to do with language.

Next, look at the ending of the word, or the suffix: *-ary*. Other words that have the same suffix are *planetary*, meaning "related to planets," and *literary*, meaning "related to literature." So now you can guess that a *dictionary* is something *related to language*.

The final strategy is to look at the context of the sentence. According to the sentence, the right strategies will help you "determine the meanings of words without looking at a dictionary." Based on this information, you can assume that a dictionary is *something* you would *look at* to *determine the meanings of words*.

When the steps are broken down like this, the process of discovering the meaning of a new word might seem very time-consuming. Luckily for us, once we learn a few simple tricks, our brains can go through this entire process very quickly. This book will teach you these tricks and show you how to use them to improve your grades and your knowledge.

HOW TO USE THIS BOOK

Immediately following this section, you will find a pretest that measures your knowledge of the skills taught in this book. If you don't do very well on the pretest, don't panic. The pretest is here so you can see how much you've improved when you're finished with the book.

Following the pretest are nine skill-building chapters. Each chapter discusses one specific vocabulary skill that will be important to your learning. Although you are free to use this book however you choose, the best way to build your skills will be to go through the chapters in order. Here is a brief outline of each chapter:

Chapter 1: Laying Roots—The Building Blocks of Meaning reviews the basic unit of meaning at the heart of every word—the root.

Chapter 2: Before and After—The Power of Prefixes and Suffixes talks about how beginnings and endings can be added to root words to create new words.

Chapter 3: Amazingly Awesome Adjectives and Adverbs discusses descriptive words that are useful in adding color and flavor to writing.

Chapter 4: The Chicken versus the Egg—Synonyms and Antonyms discusses words that have similar meanings and words that have opposite meanings.

Chapter 5: Making Sense of Homonyms and Confusing Word Pairs talks about words that sound the same but have different meanings, and words that are often confused for one another.

Chapter 6: Cracking the Case with Context Clues shows how to use the other words in a sentence to understand meaning.

Chapter 7: More Than Words Can Say—Connotation and Denotation teaches you how the meaning of words can be dependent upon how they are used.

Chapter 8: *Parlez-Vous Français?* Words from Foreign Languages discusses a number of words from foreign languages that are often used by English speakers.

Chapter 9: VIWs—Very Important Words talks about words that are useful to know.

The *Express Review Guides* series also includes the following features:

➥ *Fuel for Thought*: critical information and definitions that can help you learn more about a particular topic

➥ *Practice Lap*: quick practice exercises and activities to let you test your knowledge

➥ *Inside Track*: tips for reducing your study and practice time—without sacrificing accuracy

➥ *Caution!*: pitfalls to be on the lookout for

➥ *Pace Yourself*: extra activities for added practice

Included in each chapter are practice questions and puzzles that you can use to challenge your knowledge and gauge your progress. In addition, each chapter contains helpful tips and tricks to help make learning fun.

After the chapters, a posttest is included that makes use of the different skills and words taught in the book. If you've read the book carefully and completed the practice questions, you'll be amazed at how much you've improved since the pretest!

At the end of the book are two helpful appendices. **Appendix A** contains a list of prefixes, suffixes, and root words that will help you understand words. **Appendix B** contains a list of common abbreviations and acronyms that you may come across in reading.

EXPRESS REVIEW GUIDES

Vocabulary

Pretest

The following pretest measures your knowledge of the skills that you will learn in this book. Take your time answering the questions; remember, this book is written to help you with your vocabulary skills. After you're finished, check your answers and see how you've done!

Sentence Completion

The following exercise tests your knowledge of the vocabulary words that are featured in this book. Each sentence is followed by four answer choices. Your task is to choose the answer choice that best completes each sentence.

1. Before Aaron could run for president of the student council, he had to have another student _____ him.
   a. exceed
   b. nominate
   c. reorder
   d. clarify

2. The movie's villain was so _____ that the audience booed and hissed every time he came on the screen.
   a. unenthusiastic
   b. detestable
   c. fowl
   d. atypical

3. After reading the story, our teacher asked us to _____ the main details in one sentence.
   a. facilitate
   b. summarize
   c. manufacture
   d. configure

4. Hiroshi enjoyed his meal, but I thought mine was merely _____.
   a. mediocre
   b. nauseating
   c. simplistic
   d. sublime

5. Marco really seems to understand what he reads, and he always provides a lot of _____ for the rest of the class.
   a. ambition
   b. banter
   c. insight
   d. hospitality

6. This tissue paper is so _____ that it practically falls apart when I try to write on it.
   a. bashful
   b. scintillating
   c. flammable
   d. delicate

7. When it was discovered that the captain had been poisoned, his crew became worried; luckily, the ship's doctor cured him with a(n) _____.
   a. complement
   b. diatribe
   c. siesta
   d. antidote

8. We're going on vacation for my birthday this year because it _____ with winter break.
   a. debuts
   b. concedes
   c. coincides
   d. intercedes

9. Before you _____ to the next question, you should take some time to make sure you're happy with your answers so far.
   a. proceed
   b. descend
   c. exceed
   d. eject

10. Janine's story of her adventure in Africa was so _____ that the entire room stopped talking to listen to her.
   a. enlightened
   b. engrossing
   c. calculating
   d. naïve

11. The student was accused of copying when it was discovered that there were only _____ differences between her paper and her best friend's.
   a. unimaginable
   b. acceptable
   c. audible
   d. minute

12. My first day of babysitting was an absolute _____; the kids spilled food all over the kitchen and they wouldn't listen to anything I had to say.
   a. fiasco
   b. façade
   c. siesta
   d. hypothesis

13. Thankfully, Erica's illness is not _____; the doctors say she will make a full recovery.
   a. sociable
   b. illicit
   c. mundane
   d. terminal

14. In order for the sketch artist to make a good drawing of the suspect, you must describe the suspect as _____ as possible.
   a. deliriously
   b. accurately
   c. blandly
   d. hysterically

15. The dragon terrified the villagers, but the knight was _____ in his pursuit of the beast.
   a. despicable
   b. adequate
   c. dauntless
   d. opinionated

Choose the Right Word
Circle the italicized word that best completes the sentence.

16. Before we climb the mountain, we should take (*precautions/predicaments*) so that we don't run out of food or water.

17. Everyone loves George because he's so (*acidic/amiable*).

18. The cat's (*coarse/course*) tongue felt like sandpaper on my skin.

19. When I met the supermodel in person, I was stunned by her (*blasé/captivating*) beauty.

20. The town threw a huge (*fiesta/siesta*) to welcome home the sailors.

21. I knew my father really wanted me to play baseball; I did not want to (*disappoint/appoint*) him, so I tried out for the team.

22. My dog moped around in a state of (*melancholy/euphoria*) after my older brother left for college.

23. I couldn't read my friend's writing, so I asked him to (*deduce/clarify*) it for me.

24. The (*scalding/temperate*) hot soup had to cool down before I could eat it.

25. My CD player is very old, but I don't want to get rid of it because it is still (*despicable/functional*).

26. Our school took a field trip to the state (*capital/capitol*) building in February.

27. Ms. Gonzalez was so moved by the play that she rose to her feet and shouted "(*bravo/bon voyage*)!"

28. I sealed the letter in an (*envelop/envelope*) and put it in the mailbox.

29. That (*incessant/eloquent*) beeping is driving me crazy; would you please shut off your alarm clock?

30. Mrs. Brown will not (*accept/except*) any homework that is turned in late.

Matching Synonyms

Match the word in the first column with its synonym in the second column.
(**Synonyms** are words that have the same meaning.)

31. gaunt		**a.** dull
32. rendezvous		**b.** sharp
33. steadfast		**c.** bulky
34. kaput		**d.** speaker
35. current		**e.** thin
36. cumbersome		**f.** appetizers
37. realistic		**g.** rigid
38. acute		**h.** rule
39. tome		**i.** shy
40. bygone		**j.** book
41. bland		**k.** past
42. reign		**l.** modern
43. hors d'oeuvres		**m.** broken
44. bashful		**n.** meeting
45. lecturer		**o.** believable

Matching Antonyms

Match the word in the first column with its antonym in the second column.
(**Antonyms** are words that have opposite meanings.)

46. conscious   **a.** interesting

47. stationary   **b.** dark

48. luminous   **c.** fix

49. suffix   **d.** bold

50. cautious   **e.** sane

51. impair   **f.** lovable

52. illicit   **g.** honest

53. frugal   **h.** literal

54. monotonous   **i.** unconscious

55. multiple   **j.** moving

56. hysterical   **k.** prefix

57. authentic   **l.** once

58. treacherous   **m.** legal

59. figurative   **n.** wasteful

60. loathsome   **o.** fake

ANSWERS

Sentence Completion

1. **b. nominate.** To find the correct answer, it is helpful to know that the root *nom* means "name." Learn more about root words by reading Chapter 1.

2. **b. detestable.** Someone who is *detestable* is very unlikable. You can learn other synonyms for the word *detestable* in Chapter 4.

3. **b. summarize.** To *summarize* a story is to tell the main ideas of a story in a few words or sentences. *Summarize* is a word that is often used in school. You can learn more about important school-related words in Chapter 9.

4. **a. mediocre.** If something is *mediocre*, it is very plain and unexciting. *Mediocre* is one of the adjectives you will learn in Chapter 3.

5. **c. insight.** Someone who has *insight* into a subject really understands that subject. *Insight* is often confused with the word *incite*, which means "to provoke." Learn more about other homonyms and commonly confused words in Chapter 5.

6. **d. delicate.** *Delicate* is a synonym for *fragile*, meaning "easily broken." *Delicate* is one of the adjectives you will learn in Chapter 3.

7. **d. antidote.** An *antidote* is a potion or medicine that works against a disease or poison. As you will learn in Chapter 2, the prefix for *antidote* is *anti-*, meaning "against."

8. **c. coincides.** When two events happen at the same time, they *coincide*. *Coincide* is one of the words you will learn when you read about context clues in Chapter 6.

9. **a. proceed.** To *proceed* is to move forward. The word *proceed* is sometimes confused with the word *precede*, which means "to come before." These and other commonly confused words are discussed in Chapter 5.

10. **b. engrossing.** An *engrossing* story is so fascinating that you can't wait to hear what happens next. *Engrossing* is discussed in Chapter 7.

11. **d. minute.** The root *min* means "small." A *minute* difference is a small, almost unnoticeable difference. You will learn about the root *min* and other roots in Chapter 1.

12. **a. fiasco.** A *fiasco* is something that's gone horribly wrong. *Fiasco* is an Italian word that you will learn about when you read Chapter 8 on words from foreign languages.

13. **d. terminal.** A disease that is *terminal* is life-threatening. *Terminal* and *life-threatening* are synonyms you will learn in Chapter 4.

14. **b. accurately.** To describe someone *accurately* is to describe what he or she really looks like. The word *accurately* is discussed in Chapter 3.

15. **c. dauntless.** A knight who is *dauntless* would show great bravery. Chapter 6 shows you how to use context clues to uncover the meaning of words like *dauntless*.

Choose the Right Word

16. **precautions.** (Chapter 2) *Precautions* are steps taken to prepare ahead of time, while a *predicament* is a problem. The best choice for this sentence is *precautions*.

17. **amiable.** (Chapter 1) Someone who is *amiable* is very nice. Someone or something that is *acidic* is bitter. If everyone likes George, it is more likely that he is *amiable*.

18. **coarse.** (Chapter 5) *Coarse* and *course* are homonyms, which are words that are pronounced the same way. *Coarse* means "rough," while a *course* is a route or a class. The best word here is *coarse*.

19. **captivating.** (Chapter 3) Something that is *captivating* is unbelievably impressive. *Blasé* is a French word meaning "ordinary." A supermodel would more likely have *captivating* beauty.

20. **fiesta.** (Chapter 8) A *fiesta* is a big party, while a *siesta* is a nap. The best word choice here is *fiesta*.

21. **disappoint.** (Chapter 1) As you will learn in Chapter 1, *disappoint* and *appoint* have the same root. To *disappoint* someone is to let him or her down; therefore, the best choice here is *disappoint*.

22. **melancholy.** (Chapter 4) *Melancholy* means "sadness," while *euphoria* means "joy." The clue that the dog moped tells you that the best word here is *melancholy*.

23. **clarify.** (Chapter 9) To *clarify* is to make something clear, while to *deduce* means "to find the answer from a series of clues." It is likely that the friend can read his own writing, so the better answer is *clarify*.

24. **scalding.** (Chapter 4) In Chapter 4, you will learn that *scalding* is a synonym of *burning*. *Temperate*, on the other hand, means "mild." *Scalding* is the better of these two choices.

25. **functional.** (Chapter 3) Something that is *functional* works, while something that is *despicable* is worthy of hatred. The sentence implies that the CD player still works, so *functional* is the correct answer.

26. **capitol.** (Chapter 5) In Chapter 5, you will learn that the word *capitol* is spelled with an *o* when it is referring to a government building. *Capital* is an adjective meaning "most important" or "a city serving as the seat of government." The best choice here is *capitol*.

27. **bravo.** (Chapter 8) *Bravo* means "great job," and it is often said by people in audiences. *Bon voyage*, on the other hand, means "have a nice trip." Of course, Ms. Gonzalez can shout whatever she wants to at a play, but the best answer choice is *bravo*.

28. **envelope.** (Chapter 5) In Chapter 5, you will learn about words that are commonly confused with one another. *Envelop* and *envelope* are two words like this. *Envelop* is a verb, meaning "to cover completely," while an *envelope* is the thing you put a letter in. The correct word is *envelope*.

29. **incessant.** (Chapter 2) Something that is *incessant* keeps going nonstop, while *eloquent* is a word used to describe someone who is well spoken. In this case, the best answer is *incessant*.

30. **accept.** (Chapter 5) *Accept* and *except* are two words that are commonly confused. As you will learn in Chapter 5, *accept* is used as a verb, while *except* is used as a conjunction, like the words *but* and *and*. The best choice here, therefore, is *accept*.

Although Chapter 4 is all about synonyms and antonyms, the words in the two sections that follow come from all over the book. As you will learn, many words have synonyms and antonyms. Once you start learning these words, you can easily find other words that mean the same or opposite.

Matching Synonyms

31. (Chapter 6)	gaunt	**e. thin**
32. (Chapter 8)	rendezvous	**n. meeting**
33. (Chapter 3)	steadfast	**g. rigid**
34. (Chapter 8)	kaput	**m. broken**

35. (Chapter 5) current   l. modern
36. (Chapter 6) cumbersome   c. bulky
37. (Chapter 6) realistic   o. believable
38. (Chapter 1) acute   b. sharp
39. (Chapter 9) tome   j. book
40. (Chapter 9) bygone   k. past
41. (Chapter 3) bland   a. dull
42. (Chapter 5) reign   h. rule
43. (Chapter 8) hors d'oeuvres   f. appetizers
44. (Chapter 4) bashful   i. shy
45. (Chapter 9) lecturer   d. speaker

Matching Antonyms

46. (Chapter 1) conscious   i. unconscious
47. (Chapter 5) stationary   j. moving
48. (Chapter 1) luminous   b. dark
49. (Chapter 2) suffix   k. prefix
50. (Chapter 4) cautious   d. bold
51. (Chapter 6) impair   c. fix
52. (Chapter 5) illicit   m. legal
53. (Chapter 7) frugal   n. wasteful
54. (Chapter 4) monotonous   a. interesting
55. (Chapter 6) multiple   l. once
56. (Chapter 3) hysterical   e. sane
57. (Chapter 7) authentic   o. fake
58. (Chapter 4) treacherous   g. honest
59. (Chapter 9) figurative   h. literal
60. (Chapter 4) loathsome   f. lovable

Laying Roots
The Building Blocks of Meaning

The roots of a plant anchor the plant in the soil so that it can stand. A word root serves a similar function. Roots are the basic building blocks of all words. Every word either *is* a root or *has* a root. Just as a house cannot be built without a foundation, a word must have a root to give it meaning.

For example, take a look at this sentence:

The teacher's instructions were *unclear*.

You probably know that the prefix *un-* indicates an opposite, and that the word *unclear* means "not clear." In this case, the word *clear* is the root of *unclear*. The root is the word that is left when you strip away all the prefixes and suffixes from a word.

CAUTION!

WORD ROOTS ARE not always words by themselves. Roots generally come from Latin or Greek words. For example, *nat* is a Latin word root meaning "born." The word *native*, meaning "a person born somewhere," comes from this root, as does the word *prenatal*, meaning "before birth." Yet, if you used the word *nat* in place of *born*—for instance, "I was nat in America"—no one would know what you were talking about.

Confused yet? It gets more complicated. Sometimes words have more than one root. For example, the word *omnipotent* means all-powerful. *Omnipotent* is a combination of the Latin roots *omni-*, meaning "all or every," and *-potent*, meaning "power or strength." In this case, *omni* cannot stand on its own in a sentence, but *potent* is a perfectly acceptable English word.

Languages develop through slow changes over time. No one can say today why some words were taken whole from Latin and Greek sources and other words were changed. However, don't give up hope. If you memorize a small number of roots, you can unlock the meanings to a wide range of English words. (Note: A list of common roots can be found in Appendix A.)

PRACTICE LAP

Try to find the root in each of the italicized words.

1. The bridge was out, so the river was *impassable*.
   a. im
   b. pass
   c. a
   d. able

2. I am usually on time, but Jack is *chronically* late.

    a. chron

    b. chronical

    c. ally

    d. ic

3. The only way to succeed is by *striving* to do your best.

    a. str

    b. striv

    c. strive

    d. ing

4. The sailors drifted along lazily on the *tranquil* river.

    a. tra

    b. qui

    c. tranq

    d. uil

5. A *pediatrician* is a doctor who takes care of children.

    a. ped

    b. ia

    c. tri

    d. cian

Check your answers at the end of the chapter. How did you do?

YOU'RE TEARING ME APART!

As you saw in the sample questions, the best way to get to the root of a word is to break the word down into its syllables. Syllables, you might recall, are either single letters or combinations of letters that produce a single sound. The word *necessary*, for example, has four syllables—*ne-ces-sar-y*. When you pronounce the word aloud, you can feel the four different breaking points in the word.

For an example of how syllables can help you find roots, let's use the word *descendant*, meaning "one who comes from an ancestor." Start by tearing the word apart into its individual syllables. Don't worry—you won't hurt it!

The word breaks down into three parts: *de-scend-ant*. Now, what can you learn from looking at this word? As you will learn in Chapter 2, prefixes come at the beginning of a word, and suffixes come at the end of a word. The first step is to look at the beginning and end of the word and immediately decide if these beginnings and endings are prefixes, suffixes, or possible roots.

If you know your common prefixes and suffixes, you can immediately determine that *de* is not the root of the word. Many words use the prefix *de-*, meaning "the opposite of," such as *demerit* (the opposite of praise, or punishment) and *delist* (remove from listing). Likewise, you can rule out the suffix *-ant*, meaning "one who." This suffix is also very common, as we can see in words such as *servant* (one who serves) and *attendant* (one who attends).

The only part of the word left is *scend*. *Scend* is a Latin root meaning "to climb." Two words you might already know—*ascend* (to climb up) and *descend* (to climb down)—come from this same root. So, if we put the whole word back together, we get the definition "the opposite of someone who is climbing."

FUEL FOR THOUGHT

IT WILL OCCUR to a clever reader that "the opposite of someone who is climbing" is a very different definition of the word *descendant* than "one who comes from an ancestor." Well, clever reader, you are entirely correct. When you tear words apart into their specific parts, the parts do not always add up to an exact definition.

If you look at the two definitions closely, you can see that there *is* a relationship between the two definitions. In this situation, think of time as a hill. You are a descendant of your parents, and your parents are descendants of your grandparents. In terms of age, your grandparents are higher up on the hill than your parents, and your parents are higher up on the hill than you. So, you could say that you are the "opposite of someone who is climbing" the hill in relationship to your parents and grandparents.

Keep this in mind: Although it is important to be able to find the roots of words, roots are just the first key to understanding meaning. In later chapters, you will learn how to use the parts of words and the context of sentences to come up with definitions that are more precise. Roots can give you an understanding of what the word is about, but they will not always tell you the exact definition.

PRACTICE LAP

In each of the following practice questions, choose the word that shares the same root as the sample word.

6. *Audible* has the same root as
   a. auditorium.
   b. because.
   c. dribble.
   d. bagel.

7. *Nominate* has the same root as
   a. eaten.
   b. minute.
   c. hated.
   d. synonym.

8. *Disappoint* has the same root as
   a. disappear.
   b. appointment.
   c. interest.
   d. potato.

9. *Dilute* has the same root as
    a. flute.
    b. dictate.
    c. pollute.
    d. hesitate.

10. *Sympathy* has the same root as
    a. system.
    b. empathy.
    c. pattern.
    d. rhythm.

11. *Science* has the same root as
    a. conscious.
    b. once.
    c. alien.
    d. parasite.

12. *Incline* has the same root as
    a. recline.
    b. independent.
    c. cluster.
    d. twine.

Check your answers on page 24.

HOW DO YOU SPELL SUCCESS?

Sometimes, one Greek or Latin root will have several different spellings. For example, the words *exceed* ("to go beyond"), *intercede* ("to go between"), and *excess* ("to go too far") all have the same root. This root can be spelled *ced*, *ceed*, or *cess*. These roots are usually grouped together, like this: *ced/ceed/cess*.

In most cases, such as *ced/ceed/cess*, the relationships between the roots are easy to see. Sometimes, however, it is difficult to tell when roots are related. For example, *prehend* and *prise* are both variations on the same root, meaning "to take" or "to seize." With some of the more difficult combinations of roots, the only way to learn them is simple memorization.

FUEL FOR THOUGHT

TRACING THE DEVELOPMENT of language is extremely difficult. The main problem is that spoken language and written language did not develop at the same time. Many linguists (scholars who study language) believe that people began speaking more than 50,000 years ago. However, the earliest known written languages developed only 6,000 years ago. This means that language evolved for more than 44,000 years without any written historical record. Imagine you were trying to write a history report on the Great Depression, but not a single book or article was written that described what the Great Depression was. This is the challenge that linguists face when trying to uncover the origins of language.

The history of language is really the history of movement. As cultures settled new areas, it became beneficial for everyone to speak the same language. Greek is the oldest living language, and traces of Greek can be found throughout modern languages. The earliest form of English, known as Old English, came from the people who settled Great Britain in the fifth century A.D. In 1066 A.D., England was invaded and conquered by Latin-speaking Normans, who added many Latin words to Old English. The language continued to change until, in the mid- to late sixteenth century, we start to see English that is similar to the language we speak today.

MEMORY TRICKS

Another trick for remembering roots is to come up with images in your mind that are related to the roots. For example, the Latin root *ac/acr* means "sharp." This is the root for the word *acid*. If you had an *acidic* lemon, you know that it would taste very sharp. So when you see someone describe a pain as *acute*, you can guess that the pain is sharp.

The Greek root *dem* means "people." You know that a *democracy* is a government by the people. So when someone describes a disease as being an *epidemic*, you can guess that this is "a disease that affects many people."

PRACTICE LAP

For the following questions, use your knowledge of roots to determine the meaning of each word.

13. An *amiable* person is
   a. talkative, loud.
   b. truthful, honest.
   c. highly educated.
   d. friendly, good natured.

14. To *eject* someone from a meeting is to
   a. make that person leave.
   b. let that person speak.
   c. ask that person to stay.
   d. talk about that person.

15. Something that is *minute* is
   a. exciting.
   b. friendly.
   c. small.
   d. timely.

16. A *novice* computer programmer is someone who
   a. has just started learning to program computers.
   b. knows a lot about programming computers.
   c. programs computers for a living.
   d. hates programming computers.

17. *Cardiac* arrest is a medical problem that occurs in the
   a. legs.
   b. heart.
   c. brain.
   d. stomach.

18. If a police officer *interrogates* a suspect, the police officer is

    a. sending the suspect to jail.

    b. asking the suspect questions.

    c. punishing the suspect.

    d. letting the suspect go.

19. Two things that are *homogenous* are

    a. on top of one another.

    b. far from one another.

    c. touching on all sides.

    d. the same.

20. A *luminous* street is

    a. well lit.

    b. dangerous.

    c. long.

    d. colorful.

Check your answers on page 26.

CROSSING THE FINISH LINE

In this chapter, you learned that roots are the basic unit of meaning in words. When you read a word that is unfamiliar to you, you should first break the word apart into syllables and look for the root. This involves removing the prefixes and suffixes, and then thinking of other words that are similar.

You learned a few facts about roots that are helpful to keep in mind. For one thing, roots do not always match the exact definitions of words. Another important thing to keep in mind is that sometimes one root will have several different spellings. One helpful trick for memorizing roots is to create mental images that are related to the roots.

GAME TIME: FIND THE ROOT

Twenty Latin and Greek roots are hidden in the following puzzle. To make matters more difficult, the roots are listed by their descriptions. First, fill in the correct root next to its definition. You can use Appendix A as a reference. Next, circle the root in the puzzle. The roots can be found vertically, horizontally, diagonally, backward, or forward. The first one has been done for you as an example. You'll find the solution at the end of the chapter. Happy hunting!

```
D  M  L  X  C  A  T  G  F  P  W  H  K  U  N
A  F  A  U  T  O  B  Y  L  G  F  L  T  I  A
M  B  N  G  D  R  S  U  U  Y  E  U  J  N  T
C  L  S  A  M  S  C  Y  F  J  W  O  T  Z  N
D  N  E  Q  K  A  U  C  L  F  L  H  R  X  A
E  J  R  X  B  T  J  Q  U  A  R  S  J  S  S
M  O  R  P  H  V  P  M  X  O  D  O  H  E  N
A  L  M  L  S  J  W  R  A  D  A  L  S  C  A
M  T  E  O  Z  O  M  N  I  X  G  T  E  D  I
N  O  R  H  C  U  D  T  F  Q  Y  K  N  E  W
U  N  L  V  O  R  F  Z  P  R  O  V  S  E  P
F  S  M  T  O  C  S  S  D  B  E  P  S  C  H
R  P  A  S  P  A  T  P  A  T  H  Y  E  D  O
Q  O  V  H  N  P  I  E  W  P  T  J  N  E  N
G  H  O  M  O  D  X  O  V  C  O  V  T  C  E
```

1. Latin: big <u>mag/maj/max</u>

2. Greek: sound _____

3. Latin: to, toward, near _____

4. Latin: to wander _____

5. Latin: to flow _____

6. Greek: good, well _____

7. Latin: to be born _____

8. Greek: same _____

9. Greek: people _____

10. Latin: to call _____

11. Latin: to feel, to be aware _____

12. Greek: god _____

13. Greek: man, human _____

14. Latin: to go, yield, stop _____

15. Greek: self _____

16. Latin: blame _____

17. Greek: shape _____

18. Greek: time _____

19. Latin: all _____

20. Greek: feeling, suffering, disease _____

CHAPTER 1 WORD LIST

acidic (ă·'sid·ik) *adj.* having acid, bitter

acute (ă·'kyoot) *adj.* sharp

amiable ('aym·ee·ă·bĕl) *adj.* friendly and agreeable, good natured, like-able, pleasing

appoint (ă·'point) *v.* to assign to a position

audible ('awd·ĭ·bĕl) *adj.* able to be heard

auditorium (awd·ĭ·'tohr·ee·um) *n.* theater or venue

cardiac ('kahr·dee·ak) *adj.* of or related to the heart

chronically ('kron·ic·ă·lee) *adv.* habitually; constantly

conscious ('kon·shŭs) *adj.* awake, aware

democracy (dĕm·ˈahk·ruh·see) *n.* a government that is ruled by popular vote

descendant (dee·ˈsend·ănt) *n.* deriving from an ancestor

dilute (dī·ˈloot) *v.* to make thinner; to water down

disappoint (dis·ă·ˈpoint) *v.* to fail to fulfill expectations

eject (ee·ˈjĕkt) *v.* to remove; to throw out

empathy (ˈĕm·pă·thee) *n.* identification with the thoughts or feelings of another

epidemic (ĕ·pĭ·ˈdĕm·ik) *n.* a disease that affects many people

exceed (ĕk·ˈseed) *v.* to go beyond

excess (ĕk·sĕs) *n.* more than is needed

homogenous (hoh·ˈmah·jĕn·ŭs) *adj.* having the same genes

impassable (im·ˈpas·ă·bĕl) *adj.* impossible to pass

incline (ˈin·klīn) *n.* slope

intercede (in·tur·ˈceed) *v.* to come between

interrogate (in·ˈtair·oh·gayt) *v.* to ask questions of

linguist (ling·ˈwist) *n.* a scholar who studies language

luminous (ˈloo·min·us) *adj.* full of light

minute (mī·ˈnoot) *adj.* small

nominate (ˈnahm·in·ayt) *v.* to propose someone for an office or position

novice (ˈnah·vis) *n.* a person who is new at something

omnipotent (ahm·ˈni·poh·tĕnt) *adj.* all powerful

pediatrician (pee·dee·ă·ˈtri·shăn) *n.* a doctor who cares for children

pollute (pohl·ˈloot) *v.* to make dirty

recline (ree·ˈklīn) *v.* to lay down

science (ˈsy·ĕns) *n.* a branch of knowledge dealing with facts or truths

striving (ˈstrīv·ing) *v.* trying

sympathy (ˈsim·pă·thee) *n.* harmony of or agreement of feeling

synonym (sin·oh·nim) *n.* a word that means the same as another word

tranquil (tran·kwĭl) *adj.* peaceful

ANSWERS

1. **b. pass.** *Pass* comes from the Latin root *pass*, meaning "stretch or spread." Sometimes, there is not a direct relationship between the Latin meaning of a word and the English meaning. However, if you know your

prefixes and suffixes (as you will learn in the next chapter), you can often find the root through the process of elimination.

2. **a. chron.** *Chron* is a Greek root, meaning "time." In this case, it helps to know some other English words that use the root *chron*, such as *chronological* (in time order) or *chronometer* (a device for keeping track of time).

3. **c. strive.** This is a tricky one. The root of a word does not always take the same form when it is combined with suffixes and prefixes. You know from spelling rules that words sometimes drop the final *e* when combined with the ending *ing*—such as *leaving* and *surprising*.

4. **b. qui.** *Quies* is a Latin root meaning "rest" or "quiet." Using the context of the sentence, you can assume that *tranquil* probably has a similar root to *quiet*.

5. **a. ped.** *Ped* is a Latin root meaning "child" or "education." In this case, you can try to find the part of the word that conveys a unique meaning. You might recognize that the suffix *-cian* refers to what someone does, such as *physician* (one who works in medicine) or *beautician* (one who works in beauty). The suffix *-iatr* relates to doctors, as you can see in the words *psychiatry* (mind doctor) and *podiatry* (foot doctor). These two suffixes support the root of the word, which is *ped*.

6. **a. auditorium.** *Audible* and *auditorium* both share the same Latin root, *aud*, meaning "hearing or listening." Something that is *audible* is something that can be heard, and an *auditorium* is a public venue or theater.

7. **d. synonym.** Both *nominate* and *synonym* share the root *nom*, meaning "name." To *nominate* someone is to name that person as a contender, and a *synonym* is a word that shares a common meaning with another word. Remember: Just because a root is at the beginning of one word, it is not necessarily going to be in the same position in other words.

8. **b. appointment.** *Disappoint* and *appointment* both come from the Latin root *point*, meaning "to pierce or sting." To *disappoint* someone is to let that person down, while to *appoint* someone is to assign someone a position.

9. **c. pollute.** Both *dilute* and *pollute* come from the root *lut*, meaning "to wash." *Dilute* means "to weaken something or lessen its impact," while *pollute* means "to make something dirty."

10. **b. empathy.** The words *sympathy* and *empathy* come from the Greek root *path*, meaning "feeling, suffering, or disease." *Sympathy* means "to feel in harmony with someone" and literally experience the same feelings, while *empathy* means "vicariously experiencing the same feelings as another person," without actually having them.

11. **a. conscious.** *Science* and *conscious* share the Latin root *sci*, which means "to know." *Science* is the field of knowledge, while someone who is aware is said to be *conscious*.

12. **a. recline.** The words *incline* and *recline* both share the Greek root *clin*, meaning "to lean toward or bend." An *incline* is a slope, while to *recline* means "to lie down"; note that both these words share the same root.

13. **d. friendly, good natured.** The root *am* means "love." *Amiable* means "friendly and agreeable, good natured, likeable, pleasing."

14. **a. make that person leave.** The root *ject* means "to throw or to throw down." To *eject* someone from a meeting is to make the person leave the meeting.

15. **c. small.** *Minute* comes from the root *min*, meaning "small." Something *minute* is something small.

16. **a. has just started learning to program computers.** The root *nov* means "new." A *novice* is a person who is new at doing something.

17. **b. heart.** *Card* is a root meaning "heart." *Cardiac* arrest is also called a heart attack.

18. **b. asking the suspect questions.** *Interrogates* comes from the root *rog*, meaning "to ask." A police officer who is *interrogating* someone is asking that person questions.

19. **d. the same.** The Greek root *homo* means "same." Two things that are *homogenous* share the same genes, meaning they are the same.

20. **a. well lit.** The root *lum* means "light." A *luminous* street is full of light.

Find-the-Root Answer Key

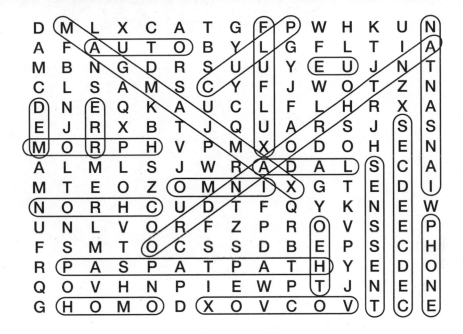

1. Latin: big <u>mag/maj/max</u>
2. Greek: sound <u>phone</u>
3. Latin: to, toward, near <u>ad/al</u>
4. Latin: to wander <u>err</u>
5. Latin: to flow <u>flu/flux</u>
6. Greek: good, well <u>eu</u>
7. Latin: to be born <u>nat/nas/nai</u>
8. Greek: same <u>homo</u>
9. Greek: people <u>dem</u>
10. Latin: to call <u>voc/vox</u>
11. Latin: to feel, to be aware <u>sens/sent</u>
12. Greek: god <u>theo</u>
13. Greek: man, human <u>anthro/andro</u>
14. Latin: to go, yield, stop <u>ced/ceed/ces</u>
15. Greek: self <u>auto</u>
16. Latin: blame <u>culp</u>
17. Greek: shape <u>morph</u>
18. Greek: time <u>chron</u>
19. Latin: all <u>omni</u>
20. Greek: feeling, suffering, disease <u>pas/pat/path</u>

Before and After
The Power of Prefixes and Suffixes

In Chapter 1, you learned all about roots, the basic unit of meaning in a word. As you may recall, the way to find the root of a word is to remove the prefixes and suffixes. "Sounds great," you may have thought, "but what in the heck are prefixes and suffixes?"

Prefixes and suffixes are syllables that carry an assigned meaning. Although prefixes and suffixes are not words on their own, they have a lot of power over words. **Prefixes** are letters that are attached to the beginning of a word, and **suffixes** are letters that are attached to the end of the word. The common name for prefixes and suffixes is **affixes**.

FUEL FOR THOUGHT

IN THE 1994 movie *The Mask*, a man finds a mask that changes his personality when he puts it on. Prefixes and suffixes behave much like this mask. They can be attached to a word and completely change that word's meaning—or, if they're feeling friendly, they can enhance the word's meaning. They can change nouns to adjectives and verbs to nouns. They can turn a *quest* into a *question* or turn an ordinary *hero* into a *superhero*. Although they don't mean much on their own, when attached to other words, affixes can make a world of difference.

PRACTICE LAP

What are the affixes in the each word?

1. disease
   a. _dis-_
   b. _ise-_
   c. _-eas_
   d. _-ase_

2. uncomfortable
   a. _un-_
   b. _un-, com-_
   c. _-fort_
   d. _un-, -able_

3. disrespected
   a. _re-, -spect, -ed_
   b. _dis-, -ed_
   c. _dis-, re-, -ed_
   d. _respect-, -ed_

4. impressive
   a. _im-, -ive_
   b. _-ive_
   c. _press-, -ive_
   d. _impre-, -ive_

5. predated
   a. _pre-_
   b. _pre-, -d_
   c. _pre-, -ed_
   d. _-d_

Check your answers at the end of the chapter. How did you do?

WORD PIONEERS

As you learned at the beginning of this chapter, prefixes are attached to the beginning of words. The word *prefix* uses a prefix itself—*pre-*, meaning "before." The prefix *pre-* changes the meaning of the root *fix.*

> *Fix*: to place securely or firmly
> *Prefix*: a group of letters placed at the beginning of a word

Although you cannot tell the meaning of a word from the prefix alone, the prefix can help you get an idea of what the word is about. For example, you might know from math class that a *polygon* is a shape with several sides. The prefix *poly-* means "many." Keeping this in mind, try to answer the following sample question:

> Someone who is *polyphobic* is
> **a.** easily excitable.
> **b.** afraid of many things.
> **c.** extremely intelligent.
> **d.** from a foreign country.

Even if you did not know that the root word *phobia* means "afraid," you can tell that the answer is choice **b**, based on your knowledge of the prefix *poly-*.

Prefixes often add valuable information to a word root. For example, the prefix *re-* means "again." If you wanted to make something for the second time, you would *remake* it. You might *reorganize* your music collection (organize it again) or *retrain* your pets (train them again). When you see the prefix *re-* at the beginning of the verb, you know immediately that, in many cases, the word will involve doing something again.

FUEL FOR THOUGHT

WHEN PREFIXES AND suffixes are shown by themselves, they are written with a hyphen. The hyphen is placed at the end of prefixes and at the beginning of suffixes, to indicate where the affix is supposed to be attached. For example, the prefix of *distress* is *dis-*. In this case, the hyphen shows that *dis-* should be placed at the beginning of a word.

PRACTICE LAP

Using your knowledge of prefixes and root words, try to determine the meaning of the words in the following questions.

6. To take *precaution* is to
   a. prepare before doing something.
   b. remember something that happened earlier.
   c. become aware of something for the first time.
   d. try to do something again.

7. To *reorder* a list is to
   a. use the same order again.
   b. put the list in a new order.
   c. get rid of the list.
   d. find the list.

8. An *antidote* to a disease is
   a. something that is part of the disease.
   b. something that works against the disease.
   c. something that makes the disease worse.
   d. something that has nothing to do with the disease.

9. Someone who is *multiethnic*
   a. likes only certain kinds of people.
   b. lives in the land of his or her birth.
   c. is from a different country.
   d. has many different ethnicities.

10. Someone who is *misinformed* has been
   a. taught something new.
   b. told the truth.
   c. forgotten.
   d. given incorrect information.

Check your answers on page 40.

MANY HAPPY ENDINGS

Like prefixes, suffixes are syllables added to words to change or enhance a word's meaning. Unlike prefixes, suffixes can be used to change a word's part of speech. For example, take a look at these sentences:

> Raoul *raced* to the finish line.
> Shana's costume was very *racy*.

In the first sentence, *raced* is a verb. In the second sentence, *racy* is an adjective. By changing the suffix from *-ed* to *-y*, the word *race* changes from a verb into an adjective.

PARTS OF SPEECH—A QUICK REVIEW

The following table offers a quick reference guide for the main parts of speech.

Part of Speech	Function	Examples
noun	names a person, place, thing, or concept	*cloud, Helen, car, Elm Court, brush, valor*
verb	shows an action, occurrence, or state of being	*go, jump, feel, imagine, interrupt*

Part of Speech	Function	Examples
adjective	describes nouns and pronouns; can also identify or quantify; tells what kind, which one, how many, how much	*white, oblong, ancient, exhilarating, that* (e.g., *that dog*), *several* (e.g., *several dogs*)
adverb	describes verbs, adjectives, other adverbs, or entire clauses; tells where, when, how, and to what extent	*slowly, clumsily, never, very, here, soon*

To see how suffixes can change parts of speech, notice how the word *adjust* is changed from a verb to an adjective to a noun.

adjust   verb   to change
                                My father had to *adjust* the brakes
                                    on the car.

adjustable adjective   able to be changed
                                The brakes on the car were *adjustable*.

adjustment noun   a change
                                My father performed an *adjustment* on the
                                    car's brakes.

INSIDE TRACK

SUFFIXES ARE REMARKABLY consistent in the parts of speech they represent. For instance, if you see the suffix *-ment*, as in *excitement* or *advertisement*, the word will always be a noun. The majority of adverbs end in *-ly*, so if you see a word with the suffix *-ly*, you can guess it is an adverb. In Appendix A, common suffixes are listed according to the parts of speech they represent.

It is important to remember that suffixes are not the same thing as word endings. The words *fly* and *silly* both end in *-ly*, yet neither is an adverb. When determining whether a word is a suffix or simply the ending of a word, it is helpful to remember your roots from Chapter 1. Remember: Suffixes and prefixes are syllables added to roots to *enhance* or *change* the root's meaning.

PRACTICE LAP

In the following questions, choose the form of the word that correctly completes the sentence.

11. Ms. Jenkins *questioned* Derek's actions. Derek's actions were
    a. questioning.
    b. questionive.
    c. questionable.
    d. questiony.

12. These baseball cards are not *worth* anything. They are completely
    a. worthy.
    b. worthless.
    c. worthible.
    d. worthing.

13. The rabbit was *nervous* around the dog. The rabbit looked at the dog
    a. nervousive.
    b. nervousless.
    c. nervousing.
    d. nervously.

14. The teacher did not *respond* to my question. She was
    a. unresponsive.
    b. responsible.
    c. respondent.
    d. responsive.

15. A group of scientists is *exploring* the North Pole. The scientists are on an
    a. exploratory.
    b. exploration.
    c. explorism.
    d. explorable.

Check your answers on page 41.

FUEL FOR THOUGHT

PREFIXES AND SUFFIXES do not have to be attached directly to a root. A word can often have more than one prefix and suffix. For instance, the word *unremarkably* has two prefixes (*un-* and *re-*) and two suffixes (*-able* and *-ly*). One of the longest words in the English language, *antidisestablishmentarianism*, has two prefixes and three suffixes: *anti-*, *dis-*, *-ment*, *-arian*, and *-ism*. Now *that's* a mouthful!

CROSSING THE FINISH LINE

In this chapter, you learned that prefixes and suffixes are known collectively as affixes. Although affixes are not words by themselves, you learned that they have a lot of power over words. Affixes are added to roots or words to change the meaning of roots or change a word's part of speech.

Prefixes are syllables that change or enhance the meanings of words. Prefixes come at the beginning of words. Suffixes are syllables that change or enhance the meanings of words or change parts of speech. Suffixes come at the end of words.

GAME TIME: FILL IN THE BLANK

Prefixes and suffixes can be attached to roots in a wide variety of ways. Your mission is to find the prefixes and/or suffixes that make each word fit the sentence. Choose from the prefixes and suffixes in the box above each set of sentences. When you are done, the remaining prefix and suffix in each box can be used to fill in the blanks of the definition of the bonus word! You'll find the solutions at the end of the chapter.

> **Box 1**
>
> re-   -ive
>
> en-   -ous
>
> de-   -ion

Congress voted to _ _act a new law that raises the minimum wage.

Rico has a very act _ _ _ imagination; he is always drawing or writing clever stories.

Sindra did not have a very good _ _act_ _ _ when I told her I couldn't come to her birthday party.

Bonus Word: shedding leaves once a year, like certain trees or shrubs: _ _ cidu _ _ _

> **Box 2**
>
> ex-   -ed
>
> in-   -or
>
> an-   -er

Jonas never _ _tend_ _ to stay later than ten; he simply lost track of time.

During the holidays, many local stores _ _tend their shopping hours.

The chimpanzee gave her baby a tend_ _ kiss on the forehead.

Bonus Word: an artist who draws cartoons: _ _ imat _ _

```
┌─────────────────────────┐
│          Box 3          │
│      pre-     -ive       │
│      sub-     -ion       │
│      dis-     -ent       │
└─────────────────────────┘
```

Jocelyn's parents sent her on a miss_ _ _ to get butter and eggs.

The king insisted that his servants be _ _ _miss_ _ _ to his orders.

Mrs. Hardy will _ _ _miss her class when the bell rings.

Bonus Word: better than all others in a particular field; world renowned: _ _ _ emin _ _ _

```
┌─────────────────────────┐
│          Box 4          │
│      con-     -ism       │
│      mal-     -ive       │
│      pro-     -ile       │
└─────────────────────────┘
```

Plastic is a more duct_ _ _ substance than wood.

Renny was very _ _ _duct_ _ _ today; she finished all her home-work right after school.

"Today, I'm going to _ _ _duct an interesting experiment," said the science teacher.

Bonus Word: misuse of a word for comic effect: _ _ _aprop_ _ _

```
┌─────────────────────┐
│       Box 5         │
│   de-      -ify      │
│   re-      -ate      │
│   in-      -ant      │
└─────────────────────┘
```

Before you send a package through the mail, you must _ _sign_ _ _ whom the package is going to on the address label.

In March, the head of the company is going to _ _sign from his position so he will have more time to spend with his family.

The driver will honk twice to sign_ _ _ that he is outside.

Bonus Word: unending: _ _ cess_ _ _

CHAPTER 2 WORD LIST

affix ('a·fiks) *n.* syllables added to the end or beginning of a word to change or enhance meaning or part of speech

animator ('a·ni·mayt·ŏr) *n.* an artist who draws cartoons

antidisestablishmentarianism ('an·tī·dis·ĕ·stab·lish·mĕn·tair·ee·ăn·ism) *n.* opposition to the belief that a country should not have an official church

antidote ('an·ti·doht) *n.* a remedy used for counteracting the effects of a disease or poison

deciduous (dee·'sid·yoo·ŭs) *adj.* shedding leaves once a year, like certain trees or shrubs

incessant (in·'sĕs·ănt) *adj.* unending

malapropism (mal·ă·'prohp·ism) *n.* misuse of a word for comic effect

misinformed (mis·in·'formd) *adj.* not informed correctly

multiethnic (muul·tī·'ĕth·nik) *adj.* having many different ethnicities

polygon ('pol·ee·gon) *n.* a shape with several sides

polyphobic (pol·ee·'fohb·ik) *adj.* frightened of many things

precaution (pree·'caw·shun) *n.* preparations taken ahead of time preeminent (pree·'ĕm·in·ĕnt) *adj.* better than all others in a particular field; world renowned

prefix ('pree·fiks) *n.* syllables that attach to the beginning of a word to change or enhance meaning

reorder ('re·or·dur) *v.* to put something in a different order

suffix ('suh·fiks) *n.* syllables that attach to the end of a word to change or enhance meaning or part of speech

ANSWERS

1. **a. dis-.** The prefix *dis-* means "away from, apart, reversal, or not." A *disease* is an illness.

2. **d. un-, -able.** The prefix *un-* means "not." The suffix *-able* means "capable or worthy of." *Uncomfortable* means "not in a state of comfort."

3. **c. dis-, re-, -ed.** The prefix *dis-* means "away from, apart, reversal, or not." The prefix *re-* means "back or again." The suffix *-ed* indicates that the word is in the past tense. *Disrespected* means "showed a lack of respect to."

4. **a. im-, -ive.** The prefix *im-* means "in, into, or within." This prefix can also be spelled *il-*, *im-*, or *ir-*. The suffix *-ive* means "having the nature of." *Impressive* means "admirable."

5. **c. pre-, -ed.** The prefix *pre-* means "before." The suffix *-ed* indicates that the word is in the past tense. *Predated* means "came before."

6. **a. prepare before doing something.** *Pre-* means "before." To take *caution* is to be careful or take heed. To take a *precaution*, therefore, is to be careful ahead of time, or to prepare before doing something.

7. **b. put the list in a new order.** If you know the meaning of the prefix *re-*, you should be able to get this one. *Re-* means "again." In this case, to *reorder* a list is to organize the list again, or put the list into a different order.

8. **b. something that works against the disease.** The prefix *anti-* means "against." In this case, if you looked for the answer choice that contained the word *against*, you picked the correct answer. An *antidote* is something that works against a disease or a poison.

9. **d. has many different ethnicities.** The prefix *multi-* means "many." Someone who is *multiethnic* has relatives from many different ethnic groups.

10. **d. given incorrect information.** *Mis-* means "opposite." To be *informed* is to have the correct information. Therefore, to be *misinformed* is to have the incorrect information.

11. **c. questionable.** In this sentence, the verb *questioned* must become an adjective. To turn the word *questioned* into an adjective, you should use the suffix *-able*.

12. **b. worthless.** The suffix *-less* means "lacking." In this case, the noun *worth* has been turned into the adjective *worthless*, meaning "not worth anything." Although choice **a**, *worthy*, is also a word, it means "worth something"; therefore, choice **b** is the best option.

13. **d. nervously.** This sentence is looking for a word to describe how the rabbit is looking. An adverb is a word that describes a verb. As you learned in this chapter, to turn a verb into an adverb, add the suffix *-ly*. The best answer, therefore, is choice **d**, *nervously*.

14. **a. unresponsive.** Remember to look at all of the clues in a test question when determining the correct answer choice. In this case, all of the answer choices are real words. However, because the sentence says the teacher did *not* respond to the question, the best answer choice is **a**. The prefix *un-* means "not," and the suffix *-ive* changes the verb *respond* into the adjective *responsive*.

15. **b. exploration.** The suffix *-tion* means "act or condition of." Scientists who are *exploring* the North Pole are on an *exploration*.

Game Time: Fill-in-the-Blank Answers

1. Congress voted to **en**act a new law that raises the minimum wage.
   Rico has a very act**ive** imagination; he is always drawing or writing clever stories.
   Sindra did not have a very good **re**act**ion** when I told her I couldn't come to her birthday party.
   Bonus Word: shedding leaves once a year, like certain trees or shrubs: **de**cidu**ous**

2. Jonas never **in**tend**ed** to stay later than ten; he simply lost track of time.
   During the holidays, many local stores **ex**tend their shopping hours.

The chimpanzee gave her baby a tend**er** kiss on the forehead.

Bonus Word: an artist who draws cartoons: **animator**

3. Jocelyn's parents sent her on a miss**ion** to get butter and eggs.

The king insisted that his servants be **sub**miss**ive** to his orders.

Mrs. Hardy will **dis**miss her class when the bell rings.

Bonus Word: better than all others in a particular field; world renowned: **preeminent**

4. Plastic is a more duct**ile** substance than wood.

Renny was very **pro**duct**ive** today; she finished all her homework right after school.

"Today, I'm going to **con**duct an interesting experiment," said the science teacher.

Bonus Word: misuse of a word for comic effect: **malapropism**

5. Before you send a package through the mail, you must **de**signate whom the package is going to on the address label.

In March, the head of the company is going to **re**sign from his position so he will have more time to spend with his family.

The driver will honk twice to sign**ify** that he is outside.

Bonus Word: unending: **incessant**

Amazingly Awesome Adjectives and Adverbs

magine, for a moment, that you had never tasted salt. French fries would taste like soggy potatoes. Popcorn would taste like cardboard. Ice cream would still taste like ice cream, because no one puts salt on ice cream. Still, even though you could eat some ice cream every now and again, you would probably feel as if something were missing from your food.

Now, one day, your friend hands you a shaker and says, "Try this." All of a sudden, a whole world of previously unimaginable* flavor opens up to you. French fries become deliriously* delicious slices of fried potatoes. Popcorn becomes a scintillating* movie-time snack. Soon, you would be wondering how you ever lived without salt in your life.

Adjectives and adverbs are the salt of language. You could get along in life perfectly well without ever using adjectives and adverbs, but you would probably always feel as if something were missing. For example, read the following paragraph:

Jonathan is a kid. He is a friend. They laugh.

Every sentence in this paragraph is grammatically correct. However, the paragraph does not say very much, nor does it make a lot of sense. The writing is bland* and functional*. In short, this paragraph is missing the salt. For comparison, take a look at this paragraph:

Jonathan is a remarkable kid. He is Cesar's best friend. They often laugh hysterically* together.

By adding a few words to each sentence, the paragraph suddenly tells you a lot more about Jonathan. Adjectives tell you what kind of kid Jonathan is (a *remarkable* kid), whose friend he is (*Cesar's*), and what kind of friend he is to Cesar (*best* friend). Adverbs tell you that Cesar and Jonathan laugh *together*, and that they laugh *often* and *hysterically*.

In the first paragraph, the sentences are rather simplistic*, placed one after another without any structure or purpose. The second paragraph, on the other hand, tells a story. Adjectives and adverbs are the descriptive words that give sentences flavor, color, and meaning.

Because adverbs and adjectives are the focus of this chapter, adjectives and adverbs (known collectively as *modifiers*) with which you may not be familiar are used throughout the chapter. These adjectives and adverbs are marked with an asterisk symbol (*). If you encounter a modifier that you do not know, turn to the glossary at the end of the chapter for a definition. Take a few minutes to learn these words when they come up . . . it will come in handy for the game at the end of the chapter!

INSIDE TRACK

Adjectives are words that modify nouns or pronouns; that is, words that describe people, places, things, or ideas. *Pretty*, *obnoxious*, and *magnificent* are all adjectives.

Adverbs are words that modify verbs, adjectives, and other adverbs. Many adverbs end in the suffix *-ly*. *Prettily*, *obnoxiously*, and *magnificently* are all adverbs.

PRACTICE LAP

In each sentence, choose the word that **cannot** be used to complete the sentence.

1. I was surprised that Jackie's new MP3 player was so _____.
    a. tiny
    b. quickly
    c. expensive
    d. fragile

2. "Let's go get some ice cream," Diego said _____.
    a. hungrily
    b. greedily
    c. excitedly
    d. hesitant

3. The new building downtown is _____ designed.
    a. imaginatively
    b. creatively
    c. ugly
    d. beautifully

4. The _____, trembling fox cowered before the angry dogs.
    a. nervous
    b. frightened
    c. scare
    d. terrified

5. The crisp mountain air smelled _____.
    a. deliciously
    b. smoky
    c. clean
    d. fresh

You'll find the answers at the end of the chapter.

RECOGNIZING ADJECTIVES

Attempting to recognize an adjective based on its spelling can be a daunting* prospect. For example, *strange*, *bizarre*, and *weird* are all adjectives. Although these adjectives all mean the same thing, there is no unifying* link in the way they are spelled that clues you in to the fact that they are all adjectives. There are, however, a few rules that can help you recognize adjectives in a sentence that you might not know.

1. Suffixes

Chapter 2 discussed suffixes that affect a word's part of speech. Suffixes such as *-able* (*manageable, adaptable, tolerable*), *-ful* (*helpful, wonderful, meaningful*), and *-y* (*sleepy, grainy, scary*) are all adjective endings. You can find a list of these suffixes in Appendix A.

2. To Be

In a sentence that uses a form of the verb *to be*, the adjective will follow the verb. This adjective always describes the subject of the sentence. Here are a few examples:

➡ I am tired.
   (*Am* is a form of *to be*; *tired* is an adjective that describes the subject *I*.)

➡ Jacquelyn and Priya were sick today.
   (*Were* is a form of *to be*; *sick* is an adjective that describes the subject *Jacquelyn and Priya*.)

➡ Be careful!
   (*Be* is a form of *to be*; *careful* is an adjective that describes the subject *you*. Although the word *you* is not in the sentence, *you* is always the implied subject in a command.)

➡ They were trying to be friendly.
   (*Were trying to be* is a form of *to be*; *friendly* is an adjective that describes the subject *they*.)

3. Sensory Verbs

Sensory verbs are verbs that are related to the senses—feel, taste, smell, sound, look, seem, and appear. In a sentence that uses a sensory verb, the adjective will follow the verb. This adjective always describes the subject of the sentence. Here are a few examples:

➡ You look ridiculous.
(*Look* is a sensory verb; *ridiculous* is an adjective that describes the subject *you*.)

➡ The television seems broken.
(*Seems* is a sensory verb; *broken* is an adjective that describes the subject *television*.)

➡ That movie sounds really good.
(*Sounds* is a sensory verb; *good* is an adjective that describes the subject *movie*. *Really* is an adverb that describes the adjective *good*.)

PRACTICE LAP

Underline the adjective(s) in each of the following sentences.

6. I felt hungry for a homemade meal.

7. We were extremely excited for the concert to begin.

8. This hamburger does not taste as delicious as I had hoped it would.

9. The angry mongoose glared menacingly at the hissing snake.

10. Sheila had a difficult time making new friends when she moved to a new town.

Check your answers on page 55.

FUEL FOR THOUGHT

IN ORDER TO truly appreciate the power of adjectives, it is helpful to think about why we use language. In the introduction to this book, we talked about how babies first start talking in words that are important to them, such as *mama*, *milk*, and *ball*. These words are all nouns. When a baby says "milk," we assume the baby is really saying, "I want some milk." But what if the baby doesn't actually want any milk, she just wants to tell her parents that she really likes milk? We have no way of knowing, because the baby has not yet learned how to use verbs.

As the baby grows, she begins to learn verbs that help her language become more specific. Now, she knows how to say, "I want milk," when she's thirsty, and "I like milk," when she just wants to talk about milk. Yes, everything is going very nicely for this baby, until one day, when she says, "I like milk," someone asks her why. The baby has no idea what to say, because the baby has not yet learned how to use adjectives. She doesn't yet know how to say, "Milk tastes good," or "milk is refreshing," or "cows are cool," because all of these statements use adjectives. All she can do is keep repeating, "I like milk."

If we only needed to tell the people around us when we wanted things, a language using nothing but nouns might be just fine. But there are so many more things we want to say to people, and this is where adjectives become incredibly useful. With adjectives, we can describe the delicate* way the sun seems to float on the ocean at sunset. We can enjoy not only a glass of milk, but also a glass of *chocolate* milk, or even a *warm* glass of *chocolate* milk, if we so desire. Knowledge and proper usage of adjectives is the key to making language specific, descriptive, and colorful.

RECOGNIZING ADVERBS

Because adverbs modify verbs, adjectives, and other adverbs, they generally tell you *how*, *why*, or *when* something is done. The best trick for finding adverbs in a sentence is to ask a question about the sentence using one of these three words and see if the sentence answers that question. For example, read this sentence:

Terrence is often late.

You can find the adverb in this sentence by asking the question, "When is Terrence late?" The answer, *often*, is an adverb. Here is another example:

Demetra is astonishingly beautiful.

In this case, the adverb can be found by asking the question, "How beautiful is Demetra?" The answer, *astonishingly*, is an adverb.

INSIDE TRACK

YOU LEARNED IN the previous chapter that adverbs often end in the suffix *-ly*. Many adverbs are adjectives with the suffix *-ly* added; for example, *beautiful* is an adjective, and *beautifully* is an adverb. *Fearless* is an adjective, and *fearlessly* is an adverb.

Some words remain the same as adjectives and adverbs. The most notable of these are the words *fast* and *hard*. In the sentence "Corinne is a fast runner," the word *fast* is an adjective. In the sentence, "Corinne runs fast," the word *fast* is an adverb.

Good and *well* are two adjectives/adverbs that are often confused. *Well* is the adverb form of the adjective *good*. In the sentence "Corinne is a good runner," the word *good* is an adjective. In the sentence "Corinne runs well," the word *well* is an adverb.

Many English speakers use the word *good* when they really mean to say *well*. The most common example is the answer to the question, "How are you?" Many people mistakenly answer this question by saying, "I am good." However, the grammatically correct answer is "I am well."

PRACTICE LAP

Underline the adverb(s) in each of the following sentences.

11. The explorers cautiously entered the ancient ruins and carefully made their way to the temple.

12. I am sometimes late for school in the morning.

13. Many people are shockingly ignorant about history.

14. It was hard to tell if Jen was working hard.

15. Although the math problem seemed ridiculously complex at first, after thinking about it for a while, I solved it easily.

Check your answers on page 56.

FUEL FOR THOUGHT

EVERY SENTENCE MUST have a subject and a verb to be considered a sentence. Although adjectives and adverbs can add layers of meaning to a sentence, at the heart of every sentence is a simple sentence without any adjectives or adverbs.

For example, the sentence *I am* is a complete sentence. *I* is the subject, and *am* is the verb. Just those two words alone are enough to be considered a sentence in the English language. This sentence, however, is basically meaningless without an adjective. In order to convey meaning, you would have to put an adjective after the *am*, such as *I am funny* or *I am hungry*. You could add an adverb to convey even more information in the sentence, such as I am *incredibly* funny or I am *usually* hungry.

GETTING INTO SPECIFICS

Unlike human beings, adjectives and adverbs are not all created equal. The strength of a description often lies in the author's ability to choose the adjective or adverb that paints the clearest picture in a reader's mind. For example, say you wanted to write a sentence about your cousin's ability to speak in public. You could say:

My cousin is a good public speaker.

This is a perfectly acceptable* sentence in the English language. However, it doesn't convey a lot of information. Although the word *good* has a positive meaning, it is not very specific. If you wanted to get more specific, you might say:

My cousin is an excellent public speaker.

A *good* public speaker might inspire polite applause after one of his speeches. An *excellent* public speaker, on the other hand, would keep the crowd's interest throughout his speech. Now, let's see what would happen if we gave your cousin even more credit:

My cousin is a captivating* public speaker.

Whoa! Now *that's* a speaker I would like to see! A *captivating* public speaker would have the audience hanging on his every word, barely daring to take a breath during his eloquent* speeches, and cheering wildly when he finishes. Simply changing the adjective turns your cousin from an average, run-of-the-mill public speaker to the kind of public speaker of whom legends are told.

Like adjectives, adverbs have varying* degrees of strength. Take a look at the following three sentences:

Johan sang well.
Johan sang beautifully.
Johan sang mellifluously*.

Mellifluous means "sweet sounding." Although it is fine to say that someone sings *well* or *beautifully*, a person who sings *mellifluously* has a gorgeous voice that truly stands out from the crowd. The strength of the adverb *mellifluously* lies in the fact that it is the most closely related to tone of voice. One can drive *well* or write *well*. One can play tennis *beautifully* or paint *beautifully*. However, singing or writing are about the only things one can do *mellifluously*.

The difference between a mediocre* adjective or adverb and a strong adjective or adverb is often subtle*. There are no steadfast* rules to determine the strongest word to use in a given situation. A good way to decide which adverb or adjective fits best is to look closely at the sentence and try to decide which adjective or adverb conveys the largest amount of information. It may seem tricky at first, but the more adjectives and adverbs you learn, the better your writing will become.

CROSSING THE FINISH LINE

In this chapter, we learned that adjectives and adverbs are descriptive words that give sentences flavor, color, and meaning. Adjectives modify nouns and pronouns, while adverbs modify verbs, adjectives, and other adverbs.

We learned that a few consistent rules apply to adjectives and adverbs. Certain suffixes, such as *-able*, -ful, *and -y*, indicate that a word is an adjective. In a sentence that uses a form of the verb *to be*, the adjective will follow the verb and describe the subject of the sentence. In a sentence that uses a sensory verb, the adjective will follow the verb and describe the subject of the sentence. A sensory verb is a verb that is related to the senses.

An adverb usually describes how, why, or when something is done. To find the adverb in a sentence, ask a question using how, why, or when. Adverbs often end in *-ly*. The adverbs *hard* and *fast* are both adjectives and adverbs. The word *good* is an adjective, while the word *well* is an adverb.

Adjectives and adverbs have differing* levels of strength. The best adjective or adverb in any given sentence is the adjective or adverb that provides the most accurate* description.

GAME TIME: CRISS-CROSS

Some adjectives and adverbs you might not have known previously were spread throughout the chapter. Choose the word from the following vocabulary list that best fits into the puzzle.

ACROSS

1. *adverb*—sounding sweet to the ear
3. *adjective*—sparkling; brilliantly clever
6. *adjective*—dull
9. *adjective*—differing by degrees
10. *adverb*—with great excitement
13. *adjective*—worthy of acceptance
14. *adjective*—fine in texture; fragile

DOWN

2. *adverb*—of moderate or barely adequate quality
4. *adjective*—in a simple or stupid manner
5. *adjective*—having differences
7. *adjective*—bringing together
8. *adverb*—consistently; correctly
11. *adverb*—crazily; in an out-of-control manner
12. *adjective*—able to capture attention
14. *adjective*—intimidating
15. *adjective*—usable

16 *adjective*—impossible to consider or believe

17 *adjective*—rigid

18 *adjective*—well spoken

CHAPTER 3 WORD LIST

acceptable (ak·′sĕp·tă·bĕl) *adj.* worthy of acceptance

accurately (′ak·ŭr·ăt·lee) *adv.* consistently; correctly

bland (bland) *adj.* dull

captivating (cap·tiv·′ayt·ing) *adj.* able to capture attention

daunting (′dawnt·ing) *adj.* intimidating

delicate (′del·i·căt) *adj.* fine in texture; fragile

deliriously (de·′leer·ee·us·lee) *adv.* with great excitement

differing (′dif·ur·ing) *adj.* having differences

eloquent (′el·oh·kwint) *adj.* well spoken

functional (′fuhnk·shăn·ăl) *adj.* usable

hysterically (his·′tair·ik·ă·lee) *adv.* crazily; in an out-of-control manner

mediocre (mee·dee·′oh·kur) *adv.* of moderate or barely adequate quality

mellifluously (mĕl·′lif·loo·us·lee) *adv.* sounding sweet to the ear

modifier (′mah·di·fi·ur) *adj.* descriptive word

scintillating (′sin·til·layt·ing) *adj.* sparkling; brilliantly clever

sensory verbs (′sĕns·or·ee ′vurbs) *n.* verbs related to the senses, including
    feel, taste, smell, sound, look, seem, and appear

simplistic (sim·′pli·stik) *adj.* in a simple or stupid manner

steadfast (′stĕd·fast) *adj.* rigid

subtle (′sut·tĕl) *adj.* delicate; difficult to detect

unifying (′yoo·ni·fi·ing) *adj.* bringing together

unimaginable (un·i·′maj·i·nă·bĕl) *adj.* impossible to consider or believe

varying (′vair·ee·ing) *adj.* differing by degrees

ANSWERS

1. **b. quickly.** This sentence is looking for a word that describes the MP3
player. *MP3 player* is a noun, which means that this sentence needs an
adjective. *Tiny*, *expensive*, and *fragile* are all adjectives. *Quickly* is an
adverb, so *quickly* is the only word that cannot be used to complete the
sentence.

2. **d. hesitant.** The best word to complete this sentence is an adverb, because it is describing something that Diego said. The only answer choice that is not an adverb is choice **d**, *hesitant*.

3. **c. ugly.** This sentence has a verb phrase (*is designed*). A word that describes a verb or verb phrase is an adverb. The only answer choice that is not an adverb is choice **c**, *ugly*. Be careful! Although many adverbs end in *-ly*, not all words that end in *-ly* are adverbs.

4. **c. nervously.** Although adverbs describe verbs, in this sentence, the comma tells you that the word being described is *fox*, a noun, and not *trembling*, a verb. Choices **a**, **b**, and **d** are all adjectives, so the only word that cannot complete the sentence is choice **c**, *nervously*.

5. **a. deliciously.** Some verbs can be followed with adverbs or adjectives, depending on the way the verb is used. In this case, the sentence is asking to describe the air, and not the process of smelling; therefore, the only choice that does not fit is choice **a**, *deliciously*.

6. I felt <u>hungry</u> for a <u>homemade</u> meal.
   Both *hungry* and *homemade* are adjectives. *Hungry* describes the word *I*, while *homemade* describes the word *meal*. Remember that *felt* is a sensory verb, and that adjectives always follow sensory verbs.

7. We were extremely <u>excited</u> for the concert to begin.
   Excited is the only adjective in this sentence. *Excited* describes the word *we*. *Extremely* is an adverb that describes the word *excited*. *Were* is a form of the verb *to be*; recall that adjectives usually follow a form of the verb *to be*.

8. This hamburger does not taste as <u>delicious</u> as I had hoped it would.
   Taste is a sensory verb, so you know that an adjective will follow it. *Delicious* is the adjective in this sentence. It describes the word *hamburger*.

9. The <u>angry</u> mongoose glared menacingly at the <u>hissing</u> snake.
   Angry, which describes the word *mongoose*, and *hissing*, which describes the word *snake*, are both adjectives. Remember that adjectives have many different verb endings.

10. Sheila had a <u>difficult</u> time making <u>new</u> friends when she moved to a <u>new</u> town.
    Difficult describes *time*, the first *new* describes *friends*, and the second *new* describes *town*. The same adjective can be used to describe two different things in a sentence.

11. The explorers <u>cautiously</u> entered the ancient ruins and <u>carefully</u> made their way to the temple.

    Cautiously and *carefully* are both adverbs in this sentence. *Cautiously* describes the verb *entered*, and *carefully* describes the verb *made*.

12. I am <u>sometimes</u> late for school in the morning.

    Sometimes is the adverb in this sentence. You can find the adverb in this case by asking the question, "When am I late?" The answer, *sometimes*, is an adverb.

13. Many people are <u>shockingly</u> ignorant about history.

    Recall that adverbs describe verbs, adjectives, and other adverbs. In this case, *ignorant* is an adjective that describes the noun *people*. *Shockingly* is an adverb that describes the adjective *ignorant*.

14. It was hard to tell if Jen was working <u>hard</u>.

    The second *hard* is the only adverb in this sentence. *Hard* is a word that is both an adjective and an adverb. In this case, the second *hard* describes how Jen is working.

15. Although the math problem seemed <u>ridiculously</u> complex at first, after thinking about it for <u>a while</u>, I solved it <u>easily</u>.

    Ridiculously, *easily*, and *a while* are the adverbs in this sentence; *ridiculously* describes the adjective *complex*, *easily* describes the verb *solved*, and *a while* describes the verb *thinking*. Remember, adverbs do not need to come directly before the word they are describing. Also keep in mind that words that answer the question "when," such as *a while*, *sometimes*, and *often*, are adverbs.

GAME TIME: CRISS-CROSS SOLUTION

Across:

1. MELLIFLUOUSLY
3. SCINTILLATING
6. BLAND
9. VARYING
10. DELIRIOUSLY
13. ACCEPTABLE
14. DELICATE

Down:

2. MEDIOCR
4. SIMP
5. DI
7. U
8. CC
11. H
12. CAPTIVATING
15. FUN
16. UNIMAGIN
17. STEADFAST
18. ELOQUENT

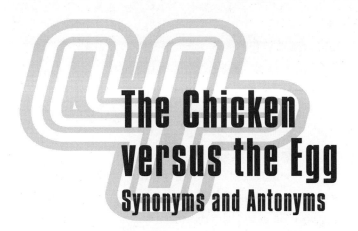

The Chicken versus the Egg
Synonyms and Antonyms

famous question asks, "Which came first, the chicken or the egg?" What the question is asking is, did the first chicken on the planet start life as a chicken, or as an egg? At first, the answer might seem obvious—chickens hatch from eggs, so the egg *must* have come first. But when you think about it a little harder, you realize that *something* had to lay the egg that the chicken came from . . . and how could there be a chicken egg if there wasn't a chicken to lay it?

Don't worry—you're not expected to know the answer to the question. Philosophers have puzzled over this issue for hundreds of years. I bring up the issue of the chicken and the egg to introduce an interesting question about language—which comes first, words or meaning? That is to say, how do we understand words without comparing them to other words?

To get an idea of what I'm talking about, look up any word in the dictionary. Just for fun, let's use the word *chicken*. If you look up the word *chicken* in the dictionary, you might see something like this:

chicken *n.* a domestic fowl

If you didn't know what a chicken was, chances are pretty good you would not know the words *domestic* or *fowl*. So when you arrived at this definition, you would probably have to look up the other two words as well.

domestic *adj.* tame

fowl *n.* a bird that is used as food

Okay, now we're getting a little bit closer. Although the definition is not perfect (pheasants, turkeys, and ducks could also be considered fowl), a chicken is most definitely a tame bird that is used as food.

So now we basically know what a chicken is. We just turned a word we didn't understand into a word we do understand by using other words for guidance. The way we learn new words is by comparing them to other words we already know. In the case of the word *domestic*, the dictionary simply gave us another word that meant the same thing—*tame*. *Tame* and *domestic* are **synonyms**. What if we didn't know the definition of the word *tame*, either? It might help to know that *tame* is the opposite of *wild*. *Tame* and *wild* are **antonyms**.

INSIDE TRACK

Synonyms are words that mean the same thing, or almost the same, as other words. The word *synonym* comes from the Greek roots *syn-*, meaning "same," and *-nym*, meaning "name." *Hard*, *difficult*, *challenging*, and *arduous* are all synonyms.

Antonyms are words that have the opposite, or nearly opposite, meaning of other words. The word *antonym* comes from the Greek roots *ant-*, meaning "opposing," and *-nym*, meaning "name." *Hard* and *easy* are antonyms.

PRACTICE LAP

In each sentence or group of sentences, choose whether the underlined words are synonyms, antonyms, or neither.

1. I think Mrs. Robinson is <u>honest</u>, but Jordan thinks she's <u>treacherous</u>.

    synonyms   antonyms   neither

2. Marley is making a <u>stew</u> for the class potluck, while Tara is cooking a <u>roast</u>.
    synonyms   antonyms   neither

3. The doctors agreed that the disease was not <u>terminal</u>. This came as welcome news to the man's family, who feared it might be <u>life-threatening</u>.
    synonyms   antonyms   neither

4. My grandfather <u>built</u> his house on the side of a mountain. He <u>erected</u> the house with his own two hands in the 1960s.
    synonyms   antonyms   neither

5. I always assumed Lisa was <u>sociable</u>; at the dance, however, she seemed rather <u>bashful</u>.
    synonyms   antonyms   neither

6. Many animals prey on rabbits, so rabbits tend to move <u>cautiously</u>. Lions do not have any natural predators, so they walk very <u>boldly</u>.
    synonyms   antonyms   neither

7. Our basement was full of old <u>junk</u>. We gathered up all the <u>trash</u> and put it in bags.
    synonyms   antonyms   neither

8. Most people in the class were <u>excited</u> to go on a field trip, but Qusai was <u>unenthusiastic</u>.
    synonyms   antonyms   neither

9. Terrah likes English class the best, while Durrell prefers Spanish.
    synonyms   antonyms   neither

10. The villagers ran for <u>safety</u> during the <u>dangerous</u> storm.
    synonyms   antonyms   neither

You'll find the answers at the end of the chapter.

PATTERNS OF BEHAVIOR

The practice questions illustrate some of the rules that apply to synonyms and antonyms. By learning these rules, you can start to identify synonyms and antonyms in sentences.

Synonyms and antonyms of a word will always share the same part of speech. The synonym and antonym of a verb will also be a verb. The synonym and antonym of an adjective will also be an adjective. A verb cannot be a synonym or antonym of a noun, an adjective cannot be the synonym or antonym of an adverb, and so on. For example, take a look at these three sentences:

I <u>love</u> pistachio pudding today, but I used to <u>hate</u> it.

I <u>love</u> pistachio pudding today, but I used to find it <u>detestable</u>.

I now think pistachio pudding is <u>delicious</u>, but I used to think it was <u>disgusting</u>.

In the first sentence, *love* and *hate* are antonyms. They are both verbs, and they mean opposite things. In the second sentence, *love* and *detestable* are not antonyms, because *love* is a verb, while *detestable* is an adjective. Even though the two words have opposite connotations (a concept we will learn more about in Chapter 7), the words must either both be verbs or both be adjectives to be considered antonyms. In the final sentence, on the other hand, *delicious* and *disgusting* are both adjectives, and therefore, they can be considered antonyms.

Not all words have synonyms or antonyms. The less specific a word is, the more likely it will have synonyms and antonyms. For example, take the sentence *He is nice. Nice* is a very general concept, and it has many different synonyms and antonyms. If you wanted to use a word besides *nice*, you could say *He is pleasant, kind-hearted, amiable,* or *considerate,* and they would all mean the same basic thing. *Pleasant, kind-hearted, amiable,* and *considerate* are all synonyms of *nice.* If you wanted to describe someone who was not nice, you could say, *He is mean, nasty, loathsome,* or *despicable,* which are all antonyms of *nice.*

More specific words are less likely to have synonyms or antonyms. For example, there is no synonym or antonym for the word *squirrel*. A squirrel is a specific animal, and there is no other word you can substitute to mean the same thing. There is also no such thing as the opposite of a squirrel.

FUEL FOR THOUGHT

SOME NOUNS DESCRIBE very specific people, places, things, or ideas. These are known as **concrete nouns**, and they tend to not have synonyms or antonyms. *Psychology*, *computer*, and *Empire State Building* are all concrete nouns. All proper nouns are concrete nouns. Proper nouns never have synonyms or antonyms.

Other nouns describe more general people, places, things, or ideas. These nouns are called **abstract nouns**, and they are more likely to have synonyms and antonyms. For example, *happiness* is an abstract noun that describes a general state of being. *Bliss*, *joy*, and *euphoria* are all synonyms of *happiness*, while *sadness*, *melancholy*, and *unhappiness* are all antonyms.

Synonyms do not always have exactly the same meanings, and antonyms are not always exact opposites. You will recall that synonyms can mean either the same thing or *almost* the same thing. *Scalding* is an adjective that means "burning." You could say that boiling water is *scalding*. You could also say that boiling water is *hot*. *Hot* and *scalding* are considered synonyms. The two words do not mean exactly the same thing, however; something that is scalding is not just hot, but *extremely* hot. A sick person's forehead might be hot, but it could not literally be scalding.

In the same manner, antonyms are not always exact opposites. *Cold* and *freezing* are both antonyms of *scalding*. Although *freezing* is closer to being an exact opposite of *scalding*, *cold* is still considered an antonym.

PRACTICE LAP

Choose the best *synonym* from the list of answer choices in each question. Remember to think about prefixes, suffixes, and roots to help uncover meanings.

11. *Transmit* means the same or almost the same as
   a. find.
   b. transplant.
   c. send.
   d. bother.

12. A word meaning the same or almost the same as *nauseating* is
   a. hungry.
   b. exciting.
   c. sickening.
   d. entirely.

13. *Function* is a synonym for
   a. attempt.
   b. time.
   c. formula.
   d. role.

14. A synonym for *devise* is
   a. create.
   b. vase.
   c. divine.
   d. tool.

15. *Monotonous* means the same or almost the same as
   a. tuneful.
   b. boring.
   c. resentful.
   d. single.

Check your answers on page 71.

RECOGNIZING ANTONYMS

Antonyms can often be recognized by their prefixes and suffixes. The next few paragraphs discuss rules that apply to prefixes and suffixes of antonyms.

Many antonyms can be created simply by adding prefixes. As you learned in the prefixes chapter, certain prefixes, such as *a-*, *de-*, *non-*, and *un-*, can be added to words to turn them into antonyms. *Atypical* is an antonym of *typical*, *deactivate* is an antonym of *activate*, *nonjudgmental* is an antonym of *judgmental*, and *unwise* is an antonym of *wise*.

Some prefixes and suffixes are antonyms of one another. The prefixes *ex-*, meaning "out of," and *in-/il-/im-/ir-*, meaning "into," are antonyms, as demonstrated by the antonym pairs *exhale/inhale*, and *explode/implode*. Other prefix pairs that indicate antonyms include *pre-/post-*, *sub-/super-*, and *over-/under-*. The suffixes *-less*, meaning "without," and *-ful*, meaning "full of," often indicate that words are antonyms, as well. For example, *meaningless* and *meaningful* are antonyms, as are *mindless* and *mindful*, and *soulless* and *soulful*.

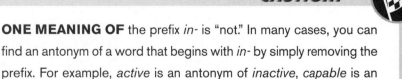

CAUTION!

ONE MEANING OF the prefix *in-* is "not." In many cases, you can find an antonym of a word that begins with *in-* by simply removing the prefix. For example, *active* is an antonym of *inactive*, *capable* is an antonym of *incapable*, and *distinct* is an antonym of *indistinct*.

Notable exceptions to this rule are the words *flammable*, meaning "able to be set on fire," and *inflammable*. If you've been paying attention so far, you might assume that *inflammable* is an antonym of *flammable*. Not so. *Flammable* and *inflammable* both mean exactly the same thing. So if you see a bottle marked *inflammable* in your chemistry class, whatever you do, keep it away from the Bunsen burner!

PRACTICE LAP

In the following questions, choose the word that is an *antonym* of the under-lined word.

16. The speaker was quite <u>responsive</u> to our questions.
    a. antiresponsive
    b. desponsive
    c. disresponsive
    d. unresponsive

17. My twin cousins are <u>distinguishable</u> from one another.
    a. indistinguishable
    b. destinguishable
    c. distinguishing
    d. prostinguishable

18. The children were <u>thankful</u> for the meal.
    a. disthankful
    b. thankless
    c. thankable
    d. inthankful

19. Jonathan was <u>prepared</u> for his speech.
    a. postpared
    b. unprepared
    c. nonprepared
    d. prepareless

20. Mr. Konami expressed his <u>pleasure</u> with our work.
    a. impleasure
    b. pleasant
    c. unpleasure
    d. displeasure

Check your answers on page 71.

INSIDE TRACK

IF YOU ARE given a set of blanks and told to fill in the correct antonyms or synonyms, it is important to consider the sentence as a whole. For example, try this practice question:

Alexis thinks Ramon is _____, but Shauna thinks he is _____.
a. brilliant; intelligent
b. generous; unselfish
c. trustworthy; unreliable
d. unpleasant; imaginative

The best answer choice in this case is choice **c**. The key to finding the best answer is in the sentence structure. The word *but* indicates that Alexis and Shauna have differing opinions; therefore, the best answer choice will be a set of antonyms. *Brilliant*; *intelligent* (choice **a**) and *generous*; *unselfish* (choice **b**) are both sets of synonyms. *Unpleasant* and *imaginative* (choice **d**) have little to do with one another. The answer, therefore, will be choice **c**, *trustworthy*; *unreliable*.

CROSSING THE FINISH LINE

In this chapter, we learned that synonyms are words that have the same or almost the same meaning, while antonyms are words that have opposite or nearly opposite meanings. We learned that synonyms and antonyms of a word will always share the same part of speech; that is, a synonym or antonym of a verb has to be a verb, a synonym or antonym of an adjective has to be an adjective, and so forth. We also learned that not all words have synonyms or antonyms, and that synonyms do not always have exactly the same meaning, and antonyms do not have to be exact opposites. Concrete nouns are nouns that describe specific people, places, things, and ideas, and they do not generally have synonyms or antonyms. Abstract nouns describe general people, places, things, and ideas, and they often have synonyms and antonyms.

Certain prefixes, such as *un-*, *non-*, and *anti-*, can be added to words to create antonyms. In addition, some prefixes and suffixes, such as *pre-/post-* and *-less/-ful*, indicate the presence of antonyms. Finally, we learned that sentence structure can be an important clue to determining whether a sentence requires synonyms or antonyms.

GAME TIME: FIND THE PALINDROME

In the following puzzle, fill in the correct word from the Chapter 4 word list found on pages 69–70. When you're done, enter the letters in the shaded boxes into the blanks below the puzzle to read a famous palindrome. (Note: A *palindrome* is a word that reads the same forward and backward.)

Palindrome: _ _ _ _, _ _ _ _ _, _ _ _ _ _ _: _ _ _ _ _ _

1. not typical
2. words that have opposite or nearly opposite meanings
3. extremely hot; burning
4. dull
5. sickening
6. mean-spirited
7. enjoying socializing
8. dishonest
9. job, role
10. unexcited
11. to build
12. difficult
13. send
14. able to be set on fire
15. worthy of hatred
16. great joy
17. shy
18. life-threatening
19. sadness
20. able to be set on fire
21. worthy of hatred

CHAPTER 4 WORD LIST

antonyms ('an·toh·nims) *n.* words that have opposite or nearly opposite
    meanings
arduous ('ahrd·yoo·us) *adj.* difficult
atypical (ay·'tip·i·kĕl) *adj.* not typical
bashful ('bash·ful) *adj.* shy
despicable (dee·'spik·ă·bĕl) *adj.* mean-spirited
detestable (dee·'tĕst·ă·bĕl) *adj.* worthy of hatred
devise (dee·'vīs) *v.* create
domestic (doh·'mĕst·ik) *adj.* tame
erect (ee·'rĕkt) *v.* to build
euphoria (yoo·'for·ee·ă) *n.* extreme happiness
flammable ('flam·mă·bĕl) *adj.* able to be set on fire

fowl (fowl) *n.* a bird that is used as food

function ('funk·shun) *n.* job, role

inflammable (in·'flam·mă·bĕl) *adj.* able to be set on fire

loathsome ('lohth·sum) *adj.* worthy of hatred

melancholy ('mĕl·ăn·ko·lee) *n.* sadness

monotonous (mă·'not·ŏn·us) *adj.* boring

nauseating ('naw·zee·ayt·ing) *adj.* sickening

scalding ('scahld·ing) *adj.* burning

sociable ('soh·shă·bĕl) *adj.* enjoying socializing

terminal ('tur·min·ăl) *adj.* life-threatening

transmit (trans·'mit) *v.* send

treacherous ('trĕ·chŭr·us) *adj.* dishonest

unenthusiastic (un·ĕn·'thoo·zi·as·tik) *adj.* unexcited

ANSWERS

1. **antonyms.** The word *but* indicates that the two ideas in the sentence will be opposing. *Treacherous*, meaning "dishonest," is an antonym of *honest*.

2. **neither.** Concrete nouns like *stew* and *roast* do not usually have antonyms or synonyms.

3. **synonyms.** *Terminal* is an adjective meaning "life-threatening"; therefore, these terms are synonyms.

4. **synonyms.** *Erected* means almost the same thing as *built*. *Built* and *erected* are synonyms.

5. **antonyms.** Someone who is *sociable* enjoys being in social situations, while someone who is *bashful* does not enjoy being in social situations. *Sociable* and *bashful* are antonyms.

6. **antonyms.** An animal that moves *cautiously* is very careful, while an animal that moves *boldly* does not take much care. In this case, you could determine these words were antonyms by the context of the sentence. You know that rabbits are scared and lions are not scared, so you can assume they would move in opposing ways.

7. **synonyms.** Although concrete nouns do not usually have synonyms or antonyms, abstract nouns often do. *Junk* and *trash* are very general nouns that both mean "unimportant stuff"; therefore, *junk* and *trash* are synonyms.

8. **antonyms.** *Excited* is a synonym for *enthusiastic*. *Unenthusiastic* is an antonym of *enthusiastic*; therefore, *excited* and *unenthusiastic* are also antonyms.

9. **neither.** *English* and *Spanish* are both proper nouns. Proper nouns do not have synonyms or antonyms, so the correct answer is neither.

10. **neither.** This is a tricky one. Antonyms and synonyms have to share the same part of speech. In this case, *safety* is a noun, while *dangerous* is an adjective. *Safety* and *danger* are antonyms, as are *safe* and *dangerous*, but *safety* and *dangerous* are not the same part of speech, and therefore, they cannot be considered antonyms.

11. **c. send.** *Trans* means "across" and *mit* means "send." A synonym for *transmit*, therefore, is *send*.

12. **c. sickening.** If someone feels *nauseous*, that person feels sick. *Nauseating* and *sickening* are synonyms.

13. **d. role.** When you talk about a tool's *function*, you are talking about its job or role; therefore, the best answer choice is **d**, *role*.

14. **a. create.** To *devise* a plan is to *create* a plan; the best answer choice is therefore choice **a**, *create*. If you picked answer choice **d**, you may have been confusing the word *devise* with the word *device*. Remember to read very carefully and make sure you understand the question before you answer!

15. **b. boring.** *Monotonous* comes from the roots *mono*, meaning "one," and *tone*, meaning "sound." Something with one sound is very boring; therefore, the best answer choice is **b**, *boring*.

16. **d. unresponsive.** *Responsive* means "eager to respond." The prefix *un-* can be added to the word *responsive* to create an antonym, *unresponsive*.

17. **a. indistinguishable.** *Distinguishable* means "able to be told apart." To create the antonym for the word *distinguishable*, add the prefix *in-*.

18. **b. thankless.** The suffixes *-less* and *-ful* are often used in antonym pairs. An antonym of *thankless* is *thankful*.

19. **b. unprepared.** Be careful. Although the prefixes *pre-* and *post-* often go together, this is not always the case. In the case of the word *prepared*, the correct antonym is choice **b**, *unprepared*.

20. **d. displeasure.** *Pleasure* is an abstract noun. To create an antonym of *pleasure*, add the prefix *dis-*. *Displeasure* (choice **d**) is the correct option.

GAME TIME: FIND-THE-PALINDROME SOLUTION

```
 1  A T Y P I C A L
 2  A N T O N Y M S
 3        S C A L D I N G
 4  M O N O T O N O U S
 5     N A U S E A T I N G
 6        D E S P I C A B L E
 7  S O C I A B L E
 8        T R E A C H E R O U S
 9        F U N C T I O N
10  U N E N T H U S I A S T I C
11        E R E C T
12           A R D U O U S
13        T R A N S M I T
14     I N F L A M M A B L E
15  D E T E S T A B L E
16        E U P H O R I A
17        B A S H F U L
18  T E R M I N A L
19     M E L A N C H O L Y
20  F L A M M A B L E
21     L O A T H S O M E
```

Palindrome: A MAN, A PLAN, A CANAL: PANAMA

Making Sense of Homonyms and Confusing Word Pairs

ead the following sentence:

There putting they're coats over their.

Does anything strike you as odd about this sentence? Take a close look. If you noticed the problem right away, then congratulations! If not, read on.

The problem, for everyone who is still reading, is that the words *there*, *they're*, and *their* are all in the wrong places. Here's how the sentence should read: They're putting their coats over there. "Why does it matter?" you might say. "The words all sound alike, anyway. If I read the sentence out loud, no one would know the words were misspelled."

You are right about this, and the example illustrates why written language can be so much more difficult than spoken language. With spoken language, there are all sorts of clues that can help you understand what the speaker is saying. If you were to ask, "Where are they putting their coats?" and someone answered, "They're putting their coats over there," you would most likely know who *they* referred to, as you were the one who asked the question, and the speaker would probably be pointing to the area referred to by *over there*. You wouldn't need to know how the three words were spelled; you'd understand perfectly well what the person was trying to tell you, thanks to all the other clues that accompany spoken language.

In written language, on the other hand, spelling counts. A few letters can sometimes make a huge difference in what a sentence is saying. For example, imagine you were writing a story about an explorer on safari in Africa. His assistant looks off into the distance and shouts, "Look out! A giant *bore* is coming!" If you told this story out loud, the audience would assume you were talking about a *boar*, a wild pig that can be very dangerous, and they would get nervous for the explorer. People reading this sentence, however, would probably just laugh, because the word *bore* means "boring person."

Words like *boar* and *bore* are considered homonyms; that is, two words that have the same pronunciation, but different meanings.

INSIDE TRACK

Homonyms are words that are pronounced the same, but have different meanings; or words that are spelled identically, but have different pronunciations and definitions.

The word *homonym* actually refers to two different terms— *homophone* and *homograph*.

Homophones are words that are spelled differently, but have the same pronunciation and different meanings. *Pear*, meaning "a kind of fruit," and *pare*, meaning "to cut," are homophones.

Homographs are words that have an identical spelling to other words, but have different meanings and different pronunciations. For example, *sewer* (soo-er), meaning "a place for waste," and *sewer* (soh-er), meaning "one who sews," are homographs.

People often use the word *homonym* to mean *homophone*; that is, words that are pronounced the same, but have different definitions, such as *pear* and *pare*. However, please be aware that homographs are considered homonyms, as well.

PRACTICE LAP

Each of the following sentences is followed by a pair of homonyms. Circle the italicized word that belongs in the sentence.

1. The cold weather was almost more than we could (*bare/bear*).

2. My grandmother bought me a lovely (*stationary/stationery*) set, in the hope that I will write her more letters.

3. My father likes to read about (*current/currant*) events.

4. This dog is testing my (*patience/patients*)!

5. The trial offered conclusive proof of the man's (*innocence/innocents*).

6. Justin couldn't decide (*weather/whether*) he liked spring or fall better.

7. Sarah is considering running for president of the student (*council/counsel*).

8. The knight set off to (*slay/sleigh*) the dragon.

9. Juan's mother doesn't like to (*medal/meddle*) in his personal life.

10. The story in the paper is certain to (*elicit/illicit*) many passionate responses from the paper's readers.

You'll find the answers at the end of the chapter.

COMMON HOMONYMS

There are hundreds of homonym pairs in the English language. The following table lists some of the more commonly confused homonym pairs.

Homonym	Brief Definition
allowed	permitted
aloud	spoken
bare (verb)	to show
bear (verb)	to withstand
beat	to hit
beet	red vegetable
board	a piece of wood
bored	uninterested
bough	tree branch
bow	to bend in a sign of respect
brake	device that stops a car or bike
break	to split apart
capital	most important; city that serves as government headquarters
capitol	government building
cell	a small room, as in a jail
sell	to trade for money
cite	to refer to
sight	vision
site	a location
coarse	rough
course	path; class
complement	match
compliment	praise
council	group of leaders
counsel	attorney, advisor
dear	beloved
deer	forest animal with antlers
die	to no longer live

Homonym	Brief Definition
dye	a substance that creates color
dual	double
duel	sword fight
elicit	to draw out
illicit	against the law
fair	considering all sides
fare	payment for travel or admittance
feat	accomplishment
feet	the things you walk on
find	locate
fined	made to pay a penalty
foreword	an introduction to a book
forward	to the front
gait	the way one walks or runs
gate	a door on a fence
grate	a frame used as a covering
great	excellent
heal	to cure
heel	the back of the foot
incite	to provoke
insight	ability to understand
lead	metal
led	guided
loan	let borrow
lone	single
overdo	do too much
overdue	late
pain	ache
pane	a panel of glass
passed	moved beyond
past	time before the present
peace	the opposite of war
piece	a part of
peal	ring
peel	the outer shell of fruit

Homonym	Brief Definition
pedal	device operated by the foot
peddle	to sell
peer	equal
pier	landing place for ships
plain	humble
plane	flying machine
principal (adjective)	main
principal (noun)	person in charge
principle	standard, moral
rain	state of weather
reign	rule
rein	rope used for steering a horse
right	correct
rite	ritual
wright	one who makes something
write	compose, as language
soar	fly
sore	in pain
stationary	still, not moving
stationery	writing paper
tail	hindmost appendage on an animal
tale	story
team	a group working together
teem	to be filled with
vain	having a large ego
vein	blood vessel
vary	to change
very	extremely
waist	area of the body above the hips
waste	misuse
who's	contraction meaning *who is*
whose	belonging to someone

NARROWING IT DOWN: CHOOSING BETWEEN HOMONYMS

When trying to choose between homonyms, sentence clues can help quite a bit. Take, for example, the words *weak* and *week*. *Weak* is an adjective, meaning "not strong," while *week* is a noun, meaning "the seven-day period between Sunday and Saturday."

I chose these words to show how you can use part of speech to determine which word belongs in a blank. For example, read the following sentence:

The swami felt (*weak/week*) after seven days of fasting.

In this example, you don't need to know that a swami is a Hindu religious leader, or that *fasting* means "to not eat for an extended period of time, often for religious reasons." Don't even worry about the "seven days" part . . . that's just put in there to trick you. No, the important thing to look at here is where the word is positioned in the sentence.

In this case, the word immediately follows the verb, *felt*. As you learned in Chapter 3, *felt* is a sensory verb, and *sensory verbs are always followed by an adjective*. Without understanding anything else in the sentence, you can determine that the correct word choice in this sentence is the adjective, *weak*.

In situations where the homonyms are each the same part of speech, it is often enough to understand the meaning of only one of the words. For example, the words *team* and *teem* are a homonym pair that is commonly used on standardized tests. You probably already know that *team* is a noun, meaning "organized group," as in a baseball team or a team of lawyers. *Team* can also be used as a verb. For example, you could say:

Every year, our school *teams* with the local television station to collect canned food for needy families.

The verb *teams* means "joins with, or unites."

The word *teem* is also a verb. Now, which word fits best in the following sentence?

During lunchtime, the cafeteria _____ (*teams/teems*) with hungry students.

The correct answer is *teems*, which means "to be filled." If you did not know the definition of the word *teems*, you could still pick it as the correct answer based on your knowledge of the word *teams*. The cafeteria is more likely to be full of hungry students than to join with hungry students.

PRACTICE LAP

Use your knowledge of sentence structure and word definitions to choose the word that best fits in the sentence.

11. The threat of a potential storm made me feel (*tense/tents*) all day.

12. A person who makes ships is known as a ship(*wright/write*).

13. Once you've hooked a fish, you have to wind the line to (*real/reel*) it in.

14. You should (*mince/mints*) the celery into tiny pieces before adding it to the stew.

15. We began our (*ascent/assent*) at the foot of the hill.

Check your answers on page 91.

COMMONLY CONFUSED WORDS

Commonly confused words are words that are not necessarily homonyms, but are often mistaken for one another. *Accept* and *except* are commonly confused words, as are *assure*, *ensure*, and *insure*; *farther* and *further*; and *loose* and *lose*. The following list shows some of the most commonly confused word pairs, along with a brief definition of each word.

Confusing Words	Brief Definition
accept	recognize
except	excluding

Confusing Words	Brief Definition
access	means of approaching
excess	extra
adapt	to adjust
adopt	to take as one's own
affect	to influence
effect (noun)	result
effect (verb)	to bring about
all ready	totally prepared
already	by this time
among	in the middle of several
between	in an interval separating (two)
assure	to make someone feel confident
ensure	to make certain
insure	to guarantee against loss or harm
beside	next to
besides	in addition to
breath (noun)	a single cycle of inhalation and exhalation
breathe (verb)	to inhale and exhale
breadth	width
disinterested	no strong opinion either way
uninterested	unengaged; having no interest in
envelop	surround
envelope	paper container for a letter
farther	beyond
further	additional
loose	not tight
lose	unable to find
may be	is a possibility
maybe	perhaps
personal	individual
personnel	employees
precede	go before
proceed	continue
proceeds	profits

Confusing Words	Brief Definition
than	in contrast to
then	next in time
who	substitute for *he*, *she*, or *they*
whom	substitute for *him*, *her*, or *them*

CASE STUDY: THE KINGS OF CONFUSION

Some of the commonly confused words you just read are very different in definition. It should be easy to remember that the only instance in which you spell the word *capitol* with an *o* is when you are referring to a governmental building; in every other instance, the word is spelled with an *a*.

Some of the words aren't that easy, however. Here are some explanations of the more confusing cases.

1. accept/except

Accept and *except* are both very common words in the English language. It may help to think of them as completely different words. It is doubtful that you would ever confuse the word *recognize* with the word *excluding*, which is really what *accept* and *except* mean. Take a look at how the two words are used in the following sentence:

> Everyone *except* George is prepared to *accept* the final results of the vote.

As the sample sentence shows, *accept* is commonly used as a verb, while *except* is commonly used in the same way as the word *but*.

Except can also be used as a verb, but its usage is very different from *accept*. The verb form of *except* means "to exclude." For example, you might say:

> *Except*ing George, we were all prepared to *accept* the final results of the vote.

When choosing between *except* and *accept*, the first thing you should do is decide which part of speech the word needs to be. If the required word should be a verb, chances are strong that the best choice will be *accept*. The only time in which *except* will be used as a verb is when it indicates that someone or something is being excluded. If the required word is *not* a verb, the correct word will always be *except*.

2. affect/effect

One of the most commonly confused word pairs is *affect* and *effect*. The words are often confused because they not only sound similar, but also have similar meanings. Just remember:

➡ *If the word is a noun, it is probably* effect. An *effect* is a result. It is often used in variations of the phrase *to have an effect* or *to have no effect*. For example, you could say:

John's speech had a powerful *effect* on the way I think about recycling.

> Or:

I keep trying to teach my dog how to roll over, to no *effect*.

Technically, *affect* can also be used as a noun, but its meaning is so specific that it is rarely used. The noun *affect* means "emotion," as distinguished from thought or action. Just remember: If the word is a noun, 99.9% of the time, *effect* will be the correct choice.

➡ *If the word is a verb, it is probably* affect. To *affect* something means to have an influence on it. For example, you could say:

The moon *affects* the tides.

> Or:

My grades were *affected* positively when I started going to sleep an hour earlier.

Effect can be used as a verb, but its usage is much less common. *Effect* as a verb means "to produce a result," as in the sentence, "Teachers try hard to *effect* changes on their students." Although this sentence is grammatically correct, more often than not, if the sentence calls for a verb, *affect* will be the correct choice.

3. assure/ensure/insure

Assure, *ensure*, and *insure* are all verbs with a similar meaning, which might lead you to believe that this means the words are interchangeable. You didn't really think it would be that easy, did you? Their meanings may be similar, but each word is used in very distinct situations.

Assure means "to make someone feel confident about something." An assurance is something one person does for another person. If you were out late at night, for example, you would call your parents to *assure* them that you would be home in time for curfew—assuming you're a good kid, of course. You might *assure* your friend that you will pay her back the $5 you borrowed from her.

Ensure means "to make certain that something will happen." You would *ensure* that you'd get home in time for curfew by leaving a few minutes early. You could also *ensure* that you brought enough warm clothes on vacation by packing your own bags.

Insure means "to guarantee against loss or harm." It is a financial term that is used with things like health insurance or life insurance. If you were an adult, you could insure your house against fire.

Be careful! People often write *insure* when they actually mean *ensure*. Unless you're discussing healthcare or financial information, it's a pretty safe bet that *ensure* is the word you should use.

4. farther/further

Even the finest authors in the world sometimes get the words *farther* and *further* confused. *Farther* and *further* are comparison words. The difference is that *farther* refers only to physical distance, while *further* refers to a relationship between two points, as in time. For example, you would say that one house is *farther* down the road than another, but you would be *further* along in a book than someone else. You can never physically go *further*, you must go *farther*. If you are referring to actual distance, *farther* is the correct word; in all other situations, *further* is correct.

5. loose/lose

There's no real reason why these two words should be confused, but they often are. They don't sound anything alike, they're totally different parts of speech, and they mean completely different things. Just remember: Something that isn't tight is *loose*. You *lose* something when you can't find it. *Loose* is an adjective, and *lose* is a verb. Enough said!

6. than/then

Than is used to compare two things. You might say that you're smarter *than* your brother, or that you like pizza better *than* spaghetti. *Then*, on the other hand, is used when referring to time. You could say, "We went to the store. *Then*, we returned home." Or, you could say, "If our teacher is ill, *then* we will have a substitute." Although the two words are spelled similarly, they are used to mean very different things.

PRACTICE LAP

Decide which commonly confused word belongs in each sentence.

16. Ms. Richards said she will still (*accept/except*) my social studies assignment, even though it's late.

17. The overwhelming smell of paint in the room made it difficult to (*breath/breathe*).

18. (*Who/Whom*) might I say is calling?

19. If you enjoy singing more (*than/then*) dancing, (*than/then*) you should quit the pompom squad and join the choir.

20. When giving a speech, it is important to thank the speaker who (*preceded/proceeded*) you.

Check your answers on page 91.

INSIDE TRACK

THE PEOPLE WHO write standardized tests have certain tricks they love to use when testing your knowledge. Homonyms are perfect fuel for people who write tests because they allow for plenty of the confusion that the test makers love. For instance, try your hand at this sample question:

To *waive* means to
a. shake your hand in greeting.
b. disobey a rule or law.
c. give up a right or claim.
d. bob up and down, like water.

As you can see, this clever question writer is working overtime to try to trick you from getting the correct answer. The right answer is choice **c**, to give up a right or claim. Did you think it might be choice **a** or choice **d**? Don't feel silly if you chose either of these answers; that's exactly what the question writer expected you to do.

On standardized tests, incorrect answers are known as **distracters**. They are called this because their entire purpose is to *distract* you from getting the right answer. A good distracter will seem as if it could be the right answer. This is where homonyms come in. Both choices **a** and **d** are definitions of the word *wave*, which is a homonym of *waive*.

If you don't know what the correct answer is, you can sometimes use the distracters to your advantage. In this case, you can assume that the answers will *not* be choice **a** or **d**, because you know that those are both definitions of the word *wave*. This leaves you with two choices, and the odds are much better that you will choose correctly if you have only two answers to choose from.

CROSSING THE FINISH LINE

Homonyms are words that have the same pronunciation but different meanings, or words that are spelled identically but have different pronunciations and definitions. When trying to find the correct homonym for a sentence, look closely at sentence clues. First, check to find the word's part of speech. If the homonyms have the same part of speech, sometimes one word can be eliminated based on definition.

Some words, such as *accept/except*, *assure/ensure/insure*, and *farther/further*, are commonly confused because of similar spellings or pronunciations. Although these words may seem similar, they often have very different meanings. Read sentences closely to determine the word that best fits each sentence.

You learned that distracters are incorrect answer choices on standardized tests. The distracters are written to seem like they may be correct. After ruling out distracters that are meant to confuse you, the possibility of choosing the correct answer improves.

GAME TIME: FIND THE HOMONYM

Each number features a definition followed by two homonyms or commonly confused word pairs from this chapter. Choose the word that best fits each definition and write that word in the box. After you're done, unscramble the letters in the shaded boxes to find a word that applies to this chapter.

1   personal
    personnel   *adj.* individual

2   counsel
    council   *n.* attorney, advisor

3   capitol
    capital   *n.* government
                  building

4 plane
plain

n. flying machine

5 complement
compliment

v. match

6 meddle
medal

v. get involved in
something against
another's will

7 weather
whether

conj. choice
between two
different options

8 breadth
breathe

n. width

9 precede
proceed

v. to continue

10 adapt
adopt

v. to take as one's own

Words that are spelled differently
but have the same pronunciation
and different meanings

CHAPTER 5 WORD LIST

ascent (as·ˈsĕnt) *n.* upward climb
assent (as·ˈsĕnt) *n.* agreement
assure (ă·ˈshŭr) *v.* to make someone feel confident
breadth (brĕdth) *n.* width
capital (ˈkap·it·ăl) *adj.* most important
capitol (ˈkap·it·ăl) *n.* government building
cite (sīt) *v.* to refer to

coarse (kors) *adj.* rough

complement ('kom·plă·mĕnt) *v.* match

compliment ('kom·plĭ·mĕnt) *v.* praise

council ('kown·sĕl) *n.* a group of leaders

counsel ('kown·sĕl) *n.* attorney; advisor

currant ('kur·ĕnt) *n.* a type of fruit

current ('kur·ĕnt) *adj.* modern, new

distracter (dis·'trakt·ur) *n.* incorrect answers on standardized tests

elicit (ĕ·'lis·it) *v.* to draw out

ensure (ĕn·'shŭr) *v.* to make certain

envelop (ĕn·'vĕl·ŏp) *v.* to surround

gait (gayt) *n.* the way one walks or runs

homographs ('hŏ·moh·grafs) *n.* words that have an identical spelling to other words but have different meanings and different pronunciations

homonyms ('hŏ·moh·nims) *n.* words that are pronounced the same as another but differ in meaning, or words that are spelled identically but have different pronunciations and definitions

homophones ('hŏ·moh·fohns) *n.* words that are spelled differently but have the same pronunciation and different meanings

illicit (il·'lis·it) *adj.* against the law

incite (in·'sīt) *v.* to provoke

insight ('in·sīt) *n.* ability to understand

insure (in·'shŭr) *v.* to guarantee against loss or harm

meddle ('mĕ·dĕl) *v.* to get involved in something against someone's will

mince (mins) *v.* to cut into tiny pieces

personnel ('pur·sŏn·nĕl) *n.* employees

precede (prĕ·'seed) *v.* to go before

principal ('prin·si·păl) *adj.* main

principal ('prin·si·păl) *n.* person in charge

principle ('prin·si·păl) *n.* standard; moral

proceed ('proh·seed) *v.* to continue

reign (rayn) *n.* or *v.* rule

rein (rayn) *n.* rope used for steering a horse

rite (rīt) *n.* ritual

site (sīt) *n.* a location

slay (slay) *v.* to kill

sleigh (slay) *n.* sled
stationary (′stay·shŏn·air·ee) *adj.* still; not moving
stationery (′stay·shŏn·air·ee) *n.* writing paper
teem (teem) *v.* to be filled with
waive (wayv) *v.* to give up a right or claim
wright (rīt) *n.* one who makes something

ANSWERS

1. The cold weather was almost more than we could **bear**.
   When used as a verb, the word *bare* means "to show," while the word *bear* means "to withstand." In this case, the sentence indicates that the cold weather is difficult to *withstand*, so *bear* is the correct answer.

2. My grandmother bought me a lovely **stationery** set, in the hope that I will write her more letters.
   Stationary means "still or not moving." Paper for writing letters is called *stationery*; therefore, *stationery* is the best answer.

3. My father likes to read about **current** events.
   A *currant* is a kind of fruit. *Current* events are events that happened recently or are continuing to happen; therefore, *current* is the correct answer.

4. This dog is testing my **patience**!
   Patients are people under medical supervision. To test someone's *patience* means to bother someone, so the best answer here is *patience*.

5. The trial offered conclusive proof of the man's **innocence**.
   Innocents is a noun, meaning "those who are innocent." *Innocence*, on the other hand, is the noun meaning "not guilty." This sentence calls for the noun that defines the concept of being free from guilt, not a person who is free from guilt.

6. Justin couldn't decide **whether** he liked spring or fall better.
   You know that the word *weather* refers to temperature and conditions in the environment. *Whether* is a conjunction that generally comes between two different options. In this sentence, *whether* is the correct answer. Be careful! You may have been fooled into picking *weather* because the sentence mentions spring and fall. Remember to keep an eye on part of speech when choosing between homonyms.

7. Sarah is considering running for president of the student **council**.
   Council and *counsel* are both nouns. *Counsel* is a word for a lawyer or an advisor, however, and *council* is a word meaning "a group of leaders." A student *council* is a group of student leaders.

8. The knight set off to **slay** the dragon.
   Sleigh is a noun, meaning "sled." This sentence calls for a verb. *Slay* is the best choice, meaning "to kill."

9. Juan's mother doesn't like to **meddle** in his personal life.
   A *medal* is an award. To *meddle* is to get involved in something against someone's will. This sentence calls for a verb; therefore, *meddle* is the best choice.

10. The story in the paper is certain to **elicit** many passionate responses from the paper's readers.
    Something that is *illicit* is illegal. To *elicit* is "to draw out." The best answer in this case is *elicit*.

11. The threat of a potential storm made me feel **tense** all day.
    To feel *tense* is "to feel anxious." The word *tents* is the plural of *tent*, which is a temporary shelter. *Tense* makes much more sense in this sentence than *tents*.

12. A person who makes ships is known as a ship**wright**.
    A person who makes ships is known as a *shipwright*. A *wright* is a builder. You know that *write* is a verb, so the word *write* can be automatically disqualified in this sentence.

13. Once you've hooked a fish, you have to wind the line to **reel** it in.
    In this case, it would help to know that a *reel* is a part of a fishing pole. However, you could figure out the correct answer if you knew that *real* is an adjective, and this sentence calls for a verb.

14. You should **mince** the celery into tiny pieces before adding it to the stew.
    Mints is the plural of *mint*. To *mince* is to cut something into tiny pieces; therefore, *mince* is the correct choice.

15. We began our **ascent** at the foot of the hill.
    This word was mentioned in an earlier chapter, in connection with the word *descendant*. To *ascend* is "to climb"; therefore, *ascent* is the correct answer choice.

16. Ms. Richards said she will still **accept** my social studies assignment, even though it's late.

Remember that if the word is a verb, *accept* is generally the correct answer choice. *Except* is almost always used as a conjunction.

17. The overwhelming smell of paint in the room made it difficult to **breathe**.

    The verb form of the noun *breath* is spelled with an *e*; therefore, *breathe* is the correct answer choice.

18. **Who** might I say is calling?

    Whom is used as a substitution for *him, her,* or *them,* while *who* is used as a substitution for *he, she,* or *they.* To find the correct answer, turn the question into a statement. You would say, "I might say *he* is calling," or "I might say *they* are calling." You would not say, "I might say *them* are calling." Therefore, the correct answer is *who*.

19. If you enjoy singing more **than** dancing, **then** you should quit the pom-pom squad and join the choir.

    Than is used when comparing two things. The first part of the sentence compares singing to dancing; therefore, *than* is the best choice. The second part of the sentence is a little trickier. The correct word is *then,* because it refers to an order in which things are done—*if* you enjoy something, *then* you should do something.

20. When giving a speech, it is important to thank the speaker who **preceded** you.

    To *proceed* is to go forward. In this case, the sentence is looking for a word that means "came before." The correct answer choice is *preceded*.

GAME TIME: FIND-THE-HOMONYM SOLUTION

1 personal
     personnel   *adj.* individual | P | E | R | S | O | N | A | L |

2 counsel
     council   *n.* attorney, advisor | C | O | U | N | S | E | L |

3 capitol   *n.* government | C | A | P | I | T | O | L |
     capital   building

4 plane
plain

n. flying machine

P L A N E

5 complement
compliment

v. match

C O M P L E M E N T

6 meddle
medal

v. get involved in
something against
another's will

M E D D L E

7 weather
whether

conj. choice
between two
different options

W H E T H E R

8 breadth
breathe

n. width

B R E A D T H

9 precede
proceed

v. to continue

P R O C E E D

10 adapt
adopt

v. to take as one's own

A D O P T

Words that are spelled differently
but have the same pronunciation
and different meanings

H O M O P H O N E S

Cracking the Case with Context Clues

In Sir Arthur Conan Doyle's classic novel *The Adventures of Sherlock Holmes*, the famed detective is talking to his assistant, Watson, about the powers of observation. Watson tells Holmes that he is constantly amazed at the detective's ability to see things that Watson had not noticed. "You see, but you do not observe," Holmes replies, to which Watson agrees.

Holmes points out one of the most important skills to being a good detective. A good detective does not just *see* the world around him or her; a good detective *observes* the world. If you are asked to look at the wall of the room you are in right now, for instance, you might just see the color of the wall and pay it no further attention. But if you look closely, you can start to pick out other things about the wall that you might not have noticed at first. There are probably marks on the wall you didn't immediately notice, or areas where the paint or wallpaper has chipped away. Does the wall have a smooth or rough surface? Is the texture shiny or dull? To find the answers to these questions, you have to look closely at the wall and really notice what it looks like, instead of simply glancing at it. This is the difference between seeing and observing.

Your ability to observe sentences closely is eminently useful when it comes to understanding new vocabulary words. For example, try this practice question with the word *eminently* from the previous sentence.

Eminently means about the same as
a. not very.
b. unfortunately.
c. unusually.
d. extremely

The best answer choice in this case is **d**, *extremely*. If you had no idea what the word *eminently* meant, you could figure it out using your powers of observation. The first thing to do is take the four answer choices and insert them back into the sentence, in place of the word *eminently*. Right away, you can rule out choice **a**, *not very*. This chapter started out talking about how useful it can be to really observe things closely. Choice **b**, *unfortunately*, doesn't make much sense either. There is nothing unfortunate about the usefulness of close observation. Choice **c**, *unusually*, does not make a lot of sense—there is nothing unusual about the statement that observing sentences closely will help you determine the meaning of vocabulary words. Given all of the choices, choice **d** is clearly the best option.

As the example shows, the best way to figure out the meaning of new vocabulary words is to become a sentence detective. One of the most important tools you can use to uncover meaning is *context*. Sentence clues that help you understand new words are called **context clues**.

INSIDE TRACK

THE WORD *CONTEXT* refers to the words and sentences that surround a word or phrase and help convey its meaning.

PRACTICE LAP

Read each sentence. Use context clues to determine the meaning of each italicized word or phrase.

1. Marcie has seen this movie once, but I have seen it *multiple* times.
   Multiple means
   a. fewer.
   b. great.
   c. several.
   d. new.

2. The two comedians are well known for their hilarious *banter* on stage.
   Banter means about the same as
   a. teasing conversation.
   b. angry fighting.
   c. graceful dancing.
   d. tender glances.

3. Blue clothing was *in vogue* last year, but it's not very popular this year.
   The phrase *in vogue* means
   a. useful.
   b. expensive.
   c. beautiful.
   d. fashionable.

4. We were very unhappy with the *haphazard* way the moving company tossed our boxes into our new house.
   Haphazard means
   a. strange.
   b. careless.
   c. efficient.
   d. entertaining.

5. My cousin began to look a little too *gaunt* after several weeks on her new diet. *Gaunt* means
   a. healthy.
   b. thin.
   c. intelligent.
   d. silly.

You'll find the answers at the end of the chapter.

DIFFERENT KINDS OF CONTEXT

There are two different kinds of context that can help you understand the meaning of new vocabulary words: *sentence context* and *situational context*.

Sentence Context

Sentence context occurs in the sentence immediately surrounding the vocabulary word. In practice questions 1–5, the context clues necessary to understand the new vocabulary words occur within the sentence. This sort of question appears often on standardized tests.

To figure out words using sentence context clues, you should first determine the most important words in the sentence. Try your hand at this example, for starters:

I had a difficult time reading the doctor's *illegible* handwriting. *Illegible* means about the same as
   a. neat.
   b. unsafe.
   c. sloppy.
   d. educated.

The first thing in this sentence that would catch the eye of a good word detective is the word *difficult*. *Difficult* is an adjective, and adjectives are very useful words when trying to understand what a sentence is saying. Next, take a look at the verb—*reading*. Already, you know that this sentence is discussing something that is *difficult* to read. Next, take a look at the word that *illegible* is describing—*handwriting*. Based on context clues, you can tell that *illegible* means the doctor's handwriting is difficult to read.

Next, look at the answer choices. Choice **a**, *neat*, can be ruled out right away. Neat handwriting would not be difficult to read. Choice **b**, *unsafe*, simply doesn't make any sense. If the doctor were flailing about and jamming her pen in patients' ears while she wrote, her handwriting might be described as *unsafe*; it takes a pretty big leap of imagination to think that this is what the sentence means, however, so we can rule out choice **b**, as well.

This brings us to the final two choices. At the risk of giving away the answer, let's start with the incorrect choice, choice **d**, *educated*. Now, it is true that doctors need to be well educated. You might have taken this answer to mean that it was difficult to read the doctor's handwriting because she used large, hard-to-understand words. Although that line of thinking is not completely off base, keep in mind that the correct answer will always be the *most likely* answer. If the doctor's handwriting is difficult to read, that most likely means that her handwriting is *sloppy*. Therefore, choice **c** is the best answer choice.

It is important to remember that test questions like this don't really test your knowledge of vocabulary. Rather, they test your ability to use context clues. If a test question asks you to figure out what a word means as it is used in a sentence, that should be your tip-off that you can use context clues to determine the meaning of a word.

FUEL FOR THOUGHT

UNDERSTANDING CONTEXT CLUES is a necessary skill for test taking. However, context clues are not always present in real written works. A writer of a magazine or newspaper article, for example, uses words that he or she knows. Oftentimes, the writer will expect his or her audience to already know these words.

If you come across an unfamiliar word while you're reading, there is absolutely nothing wrong with looking up that word in the dictionary. It can be helpful to make lists of new words and use these words in your own writing, until they become familiar. The more words you know, the easier it will be to figure out the meaning of other unfamiliar words you come across.

PRACTICE LAP

Read each sentence. Use context clues to determine the meaning of each italicized word.

6. Listening to music too loudly can *impair* your hearing.
Impair means
   a. damage.
   b. heighten.
   c. use.
   d. ensure.

7. The television show was scheduled to *coincide* with the Super Bowl so
that people who did not like football would have something to watch.
Coincide means
   a. happen before.
   b. occur at the same time.
   c. occur afterward.
   d. not happen.

8. The dialogue in that movie does not seem very *realistic*; I've never actually heard people talk this way.
Realistic means
   a. believable.
   b. humorous.
   c. poetic.
   d. exciting.

9. The weather has been very extreme lately, but today, it's much more
temperate.
Temperate means
   a. troubling.
   b. beautiful.
   c. cold.
   d. moderate.

10. I knew after a while that I could not possibly win the chess game, so I had to *concede* to my opponent.

Concede means

a. give up.

b. beat.

c. challenge.

d. thank.

Check your answers on page 109.

Situational Context

Read the following brief paragraph.

> As the sun began to set, Worthington thought about his situation. He was stranded on the side of a mountain, miles away from civilization, with nothing but one bottle of water and a box of matches. It was quite a *predicament*, all right.

Based on this selection, you can tell that the word *predicament* means a "dangerous situation." However, take another look at the sentence containing the word *predicament*:

> It was quite a *predicament*, all right.

Using sentence context alone, it would be nearly impossible to determine the meaning of the word *predicament*. This sentence alone lacks the context clues that might help you determine the word's meaning. To understand the meaning of the word *predicament*, you have to go beyond the immediate sentence to understand the situation in which the word *predicament* occurs; that is, you must understand the word's **situational context**.

The only real difference between sentence context and situational context is that sentence context occurs within the immediate sentence, while situational context occurs outside of the immediate sentence. On tests, you will often be able to determine the meanings of words strictly from sentence context. This is because material on tests is either written directly for the tests or chosen to meet the standards of whatever is being tested. In real-life reading situations, however, you might have to do a little more work to understand unfamiliar words. Context clues can come directly from the surrounding sentence itself as sentence context and from the surrounding paragraph as situational context, sometimes at the same time. For example, read the following sample paragraph and try to answer the question that follows:

> The crowd listened closely as the speaker launched into a passionate _diatribe_. He spoke about the evils of slavery, furiously condemning anyone who continued to support the practice.
>
> A _diatribe_ is a(n)
>
> **a.** angry speech.
> **b.** civilized discussion.
> **c.** exciting presentation.
> **d.** joyous talk.

The best answer is choice **a**, _angry speech_. Context clues for the word _diatribe_ can be found as both sentence context and situational context. Within the sentence, the knowledge that "the crowd listened closely" to a "speaker" tells us that a _diatribe_ has something to do with a speech. The clue that this speech was "passionate" lets us know that there were deep feelings behind the speech. But what sort of feelings were they? If we had only the sentence context to go on, we might guess that these feelings were _joyous_ or _exciting_. The next sentence, however, makes it clear: The speaker was speaking _furiously_. Based on a combination of sentence context and situational context, we now know that the best answer choice is **a**, _angry speech_.

CAUTION!

READING FOR STANDARDIZED tests is, in some ways, a different skill than reading for fun. A well-written book will draw you into the story, so that after a while, it no longer feels like you're reading. A good fiction writer does not want his or her readers to stumble over every word, because this makes it difficult to hold a reader's interest. Most people don't pick out books to learn new vocabulary words (except for this book, of course!); they pick out books because the stories seem like they may be interesting or engaging.

Material on standardized tests, on the other hand, is not chosen strictly for its ability to entertain. The material on standardized tests is, instead, chosen to be *challenging*. Challenging material tests your abilities in ways that fun material sometimes does not.

The most important thing to do when reading material on standardized tests is to *pay close attention*. When reading long pieces for fun, you can often skip over whole words or sections and still understand what's happening in the story. You usually can't skip over anything on standardized tests. Every word, every sentence, every paragraph is chosen for a specific purpose—to test your understanding of what you read.

TIPS FOR TESTS

There are four different ways in which context clues are often presented that can help you on tests. These are:

1. restatement
2. positive/negative
3. contrast
4. specific detail

Restatement

Restatement clues occur when the word is defined directly. The following sample question demonstrates a restatement clue:

Ms. Jones was *dauntless* in the face of danger, impressing us all with her bravery.
Dauntless means
a. difficult.
b. fearless.
c. imaginative.
d. pleasant.

Someone who demonstrates "bravery" in the "face of danger" is choice **b**, *fearless*. In this case, the context clues tell you exactly what the word means.

Positive/Negative

Positive/negative clues are clues that can tell you whether a word has a positive or negative meaning. The following sample question demonstrates a positive/negative clue:

> I was extremely happy while listening to the orchestra's *sublime* music.
> *Sublime* means
> **a.** challenging.
> **b.** exotic.
> **c.** frustrating.
> **d.** gorgeous.

The best choice here is choice **d**, *gorgeous*. Based on the knowledge that the music made the writer "extremely happy," you know that the best answer choice will be a positive word. *Challenging* and *exotic* are neutral words, while *frustrating* is a negative word. The most positive word of the four is *gorgeous*, which makes choice **d** the best answer option.

Contrast

Contrast clues are clues that include the opposite meaning of a word. The following sample question demonstrates a contrast clue:

> Jonas did not train very hard for the race, but Terrence was on a *rigorous* running schedule.
> *Rigorous* means
> **a.** strict.
> **b.** loose.
> **c.** boring.
> **d.** strange.

Words like *but*, *on the other hand*, and *however* are tip-offs that a sentence contains a contrast clue. In this case, we know that Terrence trained in a different way than Jonas. If Jonas did not train very hard, then Terrence trained hard for the race. The best answer here, therefore, is choice **a**, *strict*.

Specific Detail

Specific detail clues give a specific detail that can help you understand the meaning of the word. The following sample question demonstrates a specific detail clue:

The package was so heavy to carry that it became rather *cumbersome*. Something that is *cumbersome* is a(n)
a. box.
b. burden.
c. obligation.
d. gift.

To answer this question, you should look for the specific detail that is given about the package. Although a package may be contained in a *box* (choice **a**), or it may be a *gift* (choice **d**), remember that the best answer will always be the most likely choice. Choice **c**, *obligation*, is close to the meaning, but there is a better answer choice. We know from sentence details that the package was cumbersome because it was so heavy to carry; something heavy to carry is a *burden*, choice **b**.

Although the four sample questions you just read each contained one sentence with a specific type of clue, in a real reading situation, these four kinds of context clues are often used in combination, spread throughout reading selections. The following example shows a combination of these different types of context clues:

Elise sometimes had a difficult time making up her mind, but in this case, she was very *decisive*. While the other children were trying to decide which ice cream flavor to get, she stepped right up to the counter and said, "Chocolate, please!"
Someone who is *decisive* is
a. confused.
b. contrary.
c. unsure.
d. certain.

In the first sentence, we learn that Elise sometimes had a difficult time making up her mind. The word *but* tells us that this sentence contains a **contrast clue**. In the next sentence, we see through a **specific detail** clue that Elise knew right away what flavor of ice cream she wanted. These clues tell us that the best answer is choice **d**, *certain*.

CROSSING THE FINISH LINE

In this chapter, we learned that context clues are the words and sentences that surround a word or phrase and help convey its meaning. There are two different kinds of context that can help you understand new vocabulary words: sentence context and situational context.

Sentence context occurs immediately in the sentence surrounding the vocabulary word. The first thing you should do when looking for context clues is determine the most important words in the sentence. Next, look at the answer choices, and determine if they make sense in the sentence.

Situational context is context that comes from understanding the situation in which a word or phrase occurs. On tests, context clues can come from a combination of sentence context and situational context.

There are four different ways in which context clues are often presented on tests: restatement, positive/negative, contrast, and specific detail. Restatement clues are clues in which the word is defined directly. Positive/negative clues are clues that tell you whether the word has a positive or negative meaning. Contrast clues are clues that include the opposite meaning of a word. Specific detail clues are clues that give a specific detail about the word. These four types of clues are often used in combination, spread throughout reading selections.

GAME TIME: SCRAMBLED CONTEXT

In each following sentence or group of sentences, the word in parentheses is scrambled. Use context clues to figure out which word from the Chapter 6 Word List (found on page 108) belongs in the sentence. After unscrambling the word, you will find that each word has one extra letter. Enter these letters in order in the blanks that follow the choices to find a famous quote by the French philosopher René Descartes.

```
__   __ __ __ __ __,   __ __ __ __ __ __ __ __ __
1    2  3  4  5  6     7  8  9  10 11 12 13 14 15

__   __ __.
16   17 18
```

1. I accidentally spilled water on my homework, which made my teacher's comments (llbligieei).

2. The winter was extremely cold, but now that it's spring, the weather is supposed to be much more (prmtteatee).

3. The books at the used bookstore were arranged in a rather (azhrahapdh) manner; there didn't seem to be any order to the titles or authors.

4. The athlete had a (rsioiruog) training schedule to get in shape for the Olympics.

5. I became aware of how dangerous our (mepetdricnan) had become when I realized we had no matches to light a fire.

6. Ms. Dench needed help loading the (bukemmersoc) boxes into her van.

7. We couldn't stop laughing at the hilarious (rabtten) between the two main characters in the film.

8. This season, my two favorite TV shows are going to (cideochin) with one another; it's going to be difficult to figure out which one to watch.

9. The hero in this book was (lmeientyne) more likeable than the villain.

10. On our field trip, we visited an extremely (cirarliest) re-creation of an early American town.

11. The (eulbmsie) sounds of the orchestra moved me to tears.

12. The tennis shoes were in (fouveg); they were so popular, it was nearly impossible to find them in stores.

13. Over the summer, Philip grew four inches. When I last saw him, he was average weight, but now he looks (tagnuo).

14. The great explorers Lewis and Clark were (staeldsnur) in their dangerous trip across the American wilderness.

15. I had a hard time choosing what I wanted for dinner, but Tony was (ievecsdie).

16. Khan said he would (decocien) the argument to me if I could prove him wrong.

17. Make sure to take the cold medicine before you go to bed; if you take it in the morning, it can (airpima) your ability to stay awake.

18. The first time Mahira was late, I didn't mind, but it became a problem when it happened (millmupte) times.

CHAPTER 6 WORD LIST

banter ('ban·tur) *n.* playful, comedic conversation

coincide ('koh·in·sīd) *v.* to occur at the same time as

concede (kon·'seed) *v.* to give in

context ('kon·tĕkst) *n.* the words and sentences that surround a word or phrase and help convey its meaning

cumbersome ('kum·bur·sum) *adj.* bulky; awkward

dauntless ('dawnt·lĕss) *adj.* unable to be intimidated

decisive (dĕ·'sī·siv) *adj.* able to decide

diatribe ('dī·ă·trīb) *n.* angry verbal attack

eminently ('ĕm·in·ĕnt·lee) *adv.* prominently; extremely

gaunt (gawnt) *adj.* extremely thin

haphazard (hap·'ha·zărd) *adj.* careless; unplanned

illegible (il·'ej·i·bĕl) *adj.* difficult to read or decipher

impair (im·'pair) *v.* damage

multiple ('mul·ti·pĕl) *adj.* more than once

observe (ob·'zurv) *v.* to pay attention to

predicament (prĕ·'dik·ă·ment) *n.* problem

realistic (ree·ăl·'ist·ik) *adj.* based on what is real

rigorous ('rig·ŏr·us) *adj.* strict

situational (sit·ŭ·'ay·shun·ăl) *adj.* dependent upon a situation

sublime (sub·'līm) *adj.* impressively grand; gorgeous

temperate ('tĕmp·ur·ăt) *adj.* mild

vogue (vohg) *n.* fashion

ANSWERS

1. **c. several.** Because you know that Marcie has seen the movie "once," you can tell that the correct answer will have something to do with numbers. Choices **b**, *great*, and **d**, *new*, can be ruled out, because they have

nothing to do with numbers. Choice **a** does not make sense, because you cannot say you have seen a movie if you have seen it less than once. The best choice is **c**, *several*.

2. **a. teasing conversation.** In order to choose the right answer, you should think about what a comedian does. A comedian is a person who tells jokes on stage. Choices **b**, **c**, and **d** probably would not be described as "hilarious," nor are they things you would expect to see a comedian doing on stage. Therefore, the best answer is choice **a**.

3. **d. fashionable.** Context clues tell you that blue clothing is not very popular this year. Last year, however, it was *in vogue*. This tells you that the phrase *in vogue* has something to do with popularity. The choice that means almost the same as popular as choice **d**, *fashionable*.

4. **b. careless.** The context clues in this sentence tell you that the speaker was "unhappy" with the way the company "tossed" the boxes into the new house. Tossing boxes does not seem very *efficient*, so choice **c** can be ruled out. It would also not be described as *entertaining*, choice **d**. It might seem *strange*, choice **a**, but remember to pick the most likely answer choice. Choice **b**, *careless*, is the best choice.

5. **b. thin.** The words *a little too* tell you that the proper word will be negative; therefore, choices **a**, *healthy*, and **b**, *intelligent*, are not the correct answer choices. Although choice **d**, *silly*, is not a positive word, it is not the best choice. The best answer choice will have something to do with dieting. The only choice that describes a result of dieting is choice **b**, *thin*.

6. **a. damage.** If you listen to music too loudly, your hearing will be affected negatively. The answer choice that means the same as being affected negatively is choice **a**, *damage*.

7. **b. occur at the same time.** According to information in the sentence, the television show was programmed so that people who did not like football would have something to watch. Based on this information, you can assume that the show will be on at the same time as the Super Bowl, which makes choice **b** the best option.

8. **a. believable.** If a sample sentence features a semicolon, it is usually an indication that one part of the sentence will give important clues about the other part. In this case, the knowledge that the speaker has "never actually heard people talk this way" tells you that *realistic* will have some-

thing to do with the believability of the dialogue. The best choice is, therefore, choice **a**.

9. **d. moderate.** The context says that the weather has been "extreme." It does not say if the weather has been extremely cold or extremely hot; therefore, choices **b**, *beautiful*, and **c**, *cold*, can be ruled out. Extreme weather is probably pretty troubling already, so it probably wouldn't be described as *more* troubling today, ruling out choice **a**. The answer we're left with is a synonym for *temperate*: choice **d**, *moderate*.

10. **a. give up.** The speaker of the sentence knows that he or she cannot win the chess game, so choice **b**, *beat*, could not be correct. If the speaker already knows he or she cannot win, then he or she has probably already challenged the opponent; therefore, choice **c** can be ruled out. Someone probably would not thank his or her opponent after losing, so choice **d** is not the best choice. The only answer left is choice **a**, *give up*.

GAME TIME: SCRAMBLED CONTEXT SOLUTION

1. I accidentally spilled water on my homework, which made my teacher's comments **illegible**. (extra letter: *i*)

2. The winter was extremely cold, but now that it's spring, the weather is supposed to be much more **temperate**. (extra letter: *t*)

3. The books at the used bookstore were arranged in a rather **haphazard** manner; there didn't seem to be any order to the titles or authors. (extra letter: *h*)

4. The athlete had a **rigorous** training schedule to get in shape for the Olympics. (extra letter: *i*)

5. I became aware of how dangerous our **predicament** had become when I realized we had no matches to light a fire. (extra letter: *n*)

6. Ms. Dench needed help loading the **cumbersome** boxes into her van. (extra letter: *k*)

7. We couldn't stop laughing at the hilarious **banter** between the two main characters in the film. (extra letter: *t*)

8. This season, my two favorite TV shows are going to **coincide** with one another; it's going to be difficult to figure out which one to watch. (extra letter: *h*)

9. The hero in this book was **eminently** more likeable than the villain. (extra letter: *e*)

10. On our field trip, we visited an extremely **realistic** re-creation of an early American town. (extra letter: *r*)

11. The **sublime** sounds of the orchestra moved me to tears. (extra letter: *e*)

12. The tennis shoes were in **vogue**; they were so popular, it was nearly impossible to find them in stores. (extra letter: *f*)

13. Over the summer, Philip grew four inches. When I last saw him, he was average weight, but now he looks **gaunt**. (extra letter: *o*)

14. The great explorers Lewis and Clark were **dauntless** in their dangerous trip across the American wilderness. (extra letter: *r*)

15. I had a hard time choosing what I wanted for dinner, but Tony was **decisive**. (extra letter: *e*)

16. Khan said he would **concede** the argument to me if I could prove him wrong. (extra letter: *i*)

17. Make sure to take the cold medicine before you go to bed; if you take it in the morning, it can **impair** your ability to stay awake. (extra letter: *a*)

18. The first time Mahira was late, I didn't mind, but it became a problem when it happened **multiple** times. (extra letter: *m*)

Quote:

I	T	H	I	N	K,	T	H	E	R	E	F	O	R	E
1	2	3	4	5	6	7	8	9	10	11	12	13	14	15

I	A	M.
16	17	18

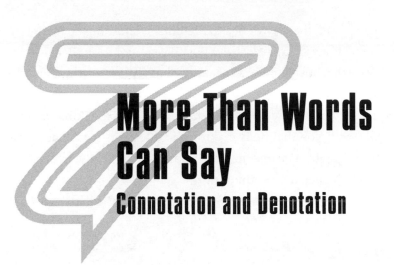

More Than Words Can Say
Connotation and Denotation

*H*ave you ever written an e-mail to someone that was taken in completely the wrong way? Maybe you were trying to write something nice to your friend, and she thought that you were making fun of her; or you were trying to say something helpful and your friend took it as criticism. This kind of confusion happens often with e-mails, because the *connotation* of e-mails is sometimes difficult to understand.

What is connotation? For an example, take a look at the following paragraph:

> "Oh, sure," Dmitri told me excitedly, "I'd just love to join your band. I bet if we practiced hard, we could become rock stars! This is going to be so exciting!"

Now, read this paragraph:

> "Oh, *sure*," Dmitri told me sarcastically, "I'd just *love* to join your band. I bet if we practiced hard, we could become rock stars! This is going to be *so* exciting!"

Although these two paragraphs differ only by a single word, that word gives them completely different meanings. The difference, of course, is in the words *excitedly* and *sarcastically*.

In the first paragraph, the knowledge that Dmitri is speaking *excitedly* tells you that he is being honest. *Excitedly* has a positive connotation. Because the word *excitedly* explains how Dmitri is speaking, that gives everything he says a positive connotation.

In the second paragraph, the knowledge that Dmitri is speaking *sarcastically* (mockingly) tells you that he is making a joke. *Sarcastically* has a negative connotation. Again, because he is speaking sarcastically, everything Dmitri says now has a negative connotation.

INSIDE TRACK

Denotation *n.* a word or text's exact meaning or dictionary definition.

Connotation *n.* a word or text's implied meaning or emotional impact.

PRACTICE LAP

Read each sentence. Following each sentence are four synonyms for the italicized word. Choose the best synonym based on the context of the sentence.

1. Sarah hung her head in shame as she slowly *walked* into the classroom.
   The best synonym for *walked* as it is used in the sentence is
   a. pranced.
   b. plodded.
   c. hiked.
   d. advanced.

2. My cousin looked very *nice* in his wedding tuxedo.
   The best synonym for *nice* as it is used in the sentence is
   a. pleasant.
   b. kind.
   c. handsome.
   d. beautiful.

3. Omar was delighted by the magician's *surprising* magic trick.

The best synonym for *surprising* as it is used in the sentence is

a. astonishing.

b. confusing.

c. bewildering.

d. alarming.

4. My grandfather will drive that beat-up old car around forever, because he's too *cheap* to buy a new one.

The best synonym for *cheap* as it is used in the sentence is

a. stingy.

b. inexpensive.

c. thrifty.

d. frugal.

5. When I asked my mother why Aunt Jacquelyn asked so many personal questions, she rolled her eyes and said, "She's always been a little too *curious*."

The best synonym for *curious* as it is used in the sentence is

a. interested.

b. weird.

c. questioning.

d. nosy.

You'll find the answers at the end of the chapter.

THE DIFFERENCE BETWEEN DENOTATION AND CONNOTATION

Common English words often have several different meanings and/or parts of speech. The word *drive*, for example, can be used as a verb or a noun. You can say someone has *a lot of drive*, meaning he or she has the will to succeed, or you can say that someone *drives to the store*, meaning he or she travels by car. You could say that someone is *driving you crazy*, in which case the word means "making." These are all different denotations of the word *drive*.

Connotation, on the other hand, is the feeling that a word creates. For example, take the first meaning of the word *drive*:

Clayton has a lot of *drive*.

Two synonyms for *drive* are the words *willpower* and *ambition*. Even though these words are technically synonyms, they both inspire different feelings. You can replace the word *drive* with these synonyms to see how words can have the same basic meaning, but different connotations.

Someone with a lot of *willpower* has the ability to fight temptation. For instance, you might say:

> Clayton has a lot of *willpower*. He loves sweets, but he stopped eating them because he wants to lose weight.

Someone with a lot of *ambition*, on the other hand, has the desire to work hard and achieve success. You could say:

> Clayton has a lot of *ambition*. He believes that if he works hard, he can someday be the president of the United States.

Each of these situations describes someone with the will to succeed. Although both words have a similar meaning, they are used in different situations. Someone who has a lot of *willpower* does not necessarily have to work hard; he or she simply has to avoid temptation. Someone with a lot of *ambition* does have to work hard, but he or she does not necessarily have to avoid temptation.

INSIDE TRACK

CONNOTATIONS OF WORDS sometimes cannot be understood simply by reading a word's dictionary definition. Connotation comes from usage. For instance, you might say you had *a blast* at a really fun party, but you would definitely not use the word *blast* to describe a party that was just kind of fun. This connotation of the word *blast* probably isn't something you were ever taught or had to look up in a dictionary; it's simply something you've learned by using the word.

One great way to learn about connotations is to pay careful attention to what you are reading, and try to understand what kind of an image the writer is creating. For example, take a look at the following two paragraphs:

Example 1

Today, the governor gave an *interesting* speech about the future of our school system. He *stated* that every teacher deserved to be paid an *adequate* wage. At the end, the audience stood and *clapped*.

Example 2

Today, the governor gave an *engrossing* speech about the future of our school system. He *proclaimed* that every teacher deserved to be paid a *comfortable* wage. At the end, the audience stood and *cheered*.

The italicized words in each paragraph are synonyms. Technically, each paragraph has the same meaning. The two examples show how much of a difference the connotations of words can make. Example 1 does not give the impression that the governor's speech was very exciting. The writer is using words with bland, neutral connotations. To the reader, the impression is that the governor gave an average speech that was greeted with mild interest. The italicized words in Example 2 have a more positive, energetic connotation than the words in Example 1. To *state* something, for instance, is to say it in a very unemotional way. To *proclaim* something is to say it in a decisive, definite manner. The impression of Example 2 is that the governor made a powerful speech that was greeted with enthusiasm by the audience.

POSITIVE, NEGATIVE, OR NEUTRAL?

When trying to decide which word is the best fit for a certain sentence, it is important to determine whether the correct word should have a *positive*, *negative*, or *neutral* connotation. The connotation of a word is determined by what you are trying to say. For example, imagine you were writing about a person you knew with a strong personality. If you liked this person, you might refer to him as *headstrong*, which has a positive connotation. If you didn't like this person, you might refer to him as *stubborn*, which has a negative connotation. If you didn't want to judge him, you might refer to him as *opinionated*, which is neutral.

PRACTICE LAP

In each of the following groups of words, one word has a negative connotation, one word has a neutral connotation, and one word has a positive connotation. Put each group of words into their correct positions in the table below. (Note: If you are not sure what some of the words mean, you can find the most difficult words defined in the Chapter 7 Word List on pages 122–123.)

	Negative	Neutral	Positive
6			
7			
8			
9			
10			

6.	mischievous	spirited	playful
7.	deserving	needy	destitute
8.	ear-splitting	loud	emphatic
9.	old	mature	decrepit
10.	calculating	knowledgeable	enlightened

Check your answers on page 124.

FUEL FOR THOUGHT

SOME WORDS COME with their connotations built right in. For example, the word *boring* is a negative word. The word *boring* simply is not used to describe someone in a positive manner. There is no occasion in which someone would say, "Boy, I really like Jack. He's so boring!"

Other words can gain connotations from the words around them. For example, take the word *predictable*, meaning "able to be known in advance." When it comes to weather, being *predictable* has a positive connotation; you know how to dress for predictable weather. When it comes to a film, however, being *predictable* has a negative connotation; with movies, we don't enjoy knowing what is going to happen ahead of time.

PRACTICE LAP

Read each sentence. Use sentence context to determine which word makes the most sense in the blank.

11. Although Ferris's mother was not happy that he broke the window, she was pleased that he was _____ about it.
    a. honest
    b. trustworthy
    c. authentic
    d. decent

12. The soldiers _____ to their feet immediately when their commander walked into the room.
    a. stood
    b. leapt
    c. rose
    d. skipped

13. Mr. Collins _____ tomatoes so vehemently that he felt ill just smelling them.
   a. resented
   b. disliked
   c. detested
   d. hated

14. The audience was practically rolling on the ground with laughter during the _____ new movie.
   a. comical
   b. humorous
   c. amusing
   d. hilarious

15. Rosa's grandparents made us feel right at home when we spent the weekend at their house with their generous _____.
   a. unselfishness
   b. politeness
   c. hospitality
   d. charity

Check your answers on page 125.

CROSSING THE FINISH LINE

In this chapter, we learned that denotation is a word or text's exact meaning or dictionary definition, while connotation is a word or text's implied meaning or emotional impact. Two words can have the same denotation and different connotations.

Connotation comes from usage. To learn connotations, it is helpful to pay attention to what you are reading and notice how the author uses words to create images.

Connotation can be positive, negative, or neutral. The correct connotation of a word is determined by the image you are trying to create.

GAME TIME: CONNOTATION CROSS-OUT

To complete this puzzle, you must first find the word from the Chapter 7 Word List on pages 122–123 that fits each definition. Then, starting at the arrow, cross out the letters of each vocabulary word, in order. When you have crossed out the letters from the definitions, place the remaining letters in order in the empty spaces below the puzzle to find a famous quote from President John F. Kennedy.

1. extremely poor: __ __ __ __ __ __ __ __ __

2. with emphasis: __ __ __ __ __ __ __ __

3. drive: __ __ __ __ __ __ __ __

4. lively: __ __ __ __ __ __ __ __

5. weakened by old age; feeble: __ __ __ __ __ __ __ __ __

6. practicing smart economic management: __ __ __ __ __ __ __

7. state definitively: __ __ __ __ __ __ __ __

8. fascinating: __ __ __ __ __ __ __ __ __ __

Quote: __ __   __ __ __ __ __ __   __ __ __ __ __ __ __ __ __ __: __ __ __

__ __ __   __ __ __ __   __ __ __ __ __ __ __   __ __ __

__ __   __ __ __   __ __ __‑__ __ __   __ __ __ __   __ __ __   __ __ __

__ __   __ __ __   __ __ __ __   __ __ __ __ __ __ __.

CHAPTER 7 WORD LIST

adequate ('ad·ĕ·kwăt) *adj.* just enough

ambition (am·'bi·shun) *n.* drive

authentic (aw·'then·tik) *adj.* real

calculating ('kal·kŭ·layt·ing) *adj.* selfishly scheming

connotation (kon·oh·'tay·shun) *n.* a word or text's implied meaning or emotional impact

decrepit (dĕ·'krep·it) *adj.* weakened by old age; feeble

denotation (dee·noh·'tay·shun) *n.* a word or text's exact meaning or dictionary definition

destitute ('dĕs·ti·toot) *adj.* poor

emphatic (ĕm·'fat·ik) *adj.* with emphasis

engrossing (en·'groh·sing) *adj.* fascinating

enlightened (en·'līt·end) *adj.* having spiritual or intellectual insight

frugal ('froo·găl) *adj.* practicing smart economic management

headstrong ('hĕd·strong) *adj.* having strong opinions

hospitality (hŏs·pi·'tal·i·tee) *n.* the friendly reception of guests and strangers

mischievous ('mis·chĕ·vus) *adj.* playfully annoying

opinionated (oh·'pin·yun·ayt·ĕd) *adj.* having strong opinions

proclaim (proh·'klaym) *v.* state definitively

sarcastically (sar·'ka·stik·lee) *adv.* mockingly

spirited ('speer·it·ed) *adj.* lively

thrifty ('thrif·tee) *adj.* practicing smart economic management

willpower ('wil·pow·ur) *n.* the ability to avoid temptation

ANSWERS

1. **b. plodded.** You know from the context that Sarah walked slowly into the room. To *prance* is to walk boldly, so choice **a** is not correct. To *hike* (choice **c**) is to walk with energy, and she probably would not walk with energy if she was filled with shame. Although *advanced* (choice **d**) is neutral, the sentence context implies that the correct word will have a negative connotation; therefore, choice **b** is the best choice.

2. **c. handsome.** You know that the speaker's cousin *looked* nice, so the best choice will either be **handsome** (choice **c**) or **beautiful** (choice **d**). The cousin is a male, and men are usually described as **handsome**; therefore, choice **c** is the best option.

3. **a. astonishing.** The knowledge that Omar was delighted by the magic trick can help you find the correct answer. Omar would most likely not be delighted by a magic trick that was *confusing* (choice **b**), *bewildering* (choice **c**), or *alarming* (choice **d**); all three of those words have negative connotations. The best answer choice in this case is choice **a**, *astonishing*.

4. **a. stingy.** Although *inexpensive* (choice **b**) is a synonym for *cheap,* in this case, you can tell by the context that *inexpensive* would not make sense in the sentence. The word *cheap* has a negative connotation. *Thrifty* (choice **c**) and *frugal* (choice **d**) are both words that describe people who don't spend much money; however, both words have positive connotations. The best answer choice is **a**, *stingy*.

5. **d. nosy.** Choice **b** (*weird*) can be ruled out first. Although *weird* is a synonym for *curious,* the context of the sentence should tell you that the proper word will have a different denotation. Based on the fact that the speaker's mother "rolled her eyes," you can determine that the proper choice will have a negative connotation. Choice **a** (*interested*) has a positive connotation, while choice **c** (*questioning*) has a neutral connotation. Therefore, the best answer choice is **d**, *nosy*.

	Negative	Neutral	Positive
6	mischievous	playful	spirited
7	destitute	needy	deserving
8	ear-splitting	loud	emphatic
9	decrepit	old	mature
10	calculating	knowledgeable	enlightened

6. To be *playful* is to enjoy playing, which does not have a negative or positive connotation. To be *mischievous* is to enjoy causing mischief, which means about the same as being a troublemaker; therefore, *mischievous* is the most negative of the three words. To be *spirited* is to be lively and courageous, which gives it a positive connotation.

7. A *needy* person is someone who needs something; *needy* does not have a negative or positive connotation. When someone is *destitute*, neediness affects his or her life negatively, so *destitute* has a negative connotation. If someone is *deserving*, it means he or she is needy but deserves more, so this word has a positive connotation.

8. The word *loud* describes a state of volume; it is not negative or positive. *Ear-splitting* sound is hard to listen to, which gives *ear-splitting* a negative connotation. If a sound is *emphatic*, however, it is loud with a purpose, which gives *emphatic* a positive connotation.

9. To say that something is *old* is a neutral statement. To describe something as *decrepit* is to imply that it is *too* old, which makes this the negative word. To describe something as *mature* is to imply that it has aged well, which makes *mature* the positive word in this group.

10. Someone who is *knowledgeable* knows about something, and this does not have a negative or positive connotation. Someone who is *calculating* uses his or her knowledge to take advantage of people, so this word has a negative connotation. Someone who is *enlightened* has become a better person thanks to his or her knowledge, so *enlightened* has a positive connotation.

11. **a. honest.** All of these words are synonyms for the word *honest*, but sometimes, the most neutral word is the best word in the sentence. In this case, *trustworthy* (choice **b**), *authentic* (choice **c**), and *decent* (choice **d**) do not make as much sense as the simplest option, choice **a**.

12. **b. leapt.** The context tells you that the soldiers stood up quickly. *Stood* (choice **a**) and *rose* (choice **c**) are neutral words that do not convey a sense of urgency. *Skipped* (choice **d**) has a positive connotation that implies the soldiers happily got their feet; *leapt* (choice **b**) is the only word that implies the urgency and immediacy demanded by the sentence context.

13. **c. detested.** The knowledge that Mr. Collins feels "ill just smelling" tomatoes suggests that his hatred for tomatoes is intense; therefore, the best choice will be the most negative. To *dislike* tomatoes (choice **b**) is the most neutral word, so this choice can be ruled out. *Resented* (choice **a**) is a word that generally applies to people or their actions, so **a** is not the best choice. Given the choice between *hated* (choice **d**) and *detested* (choice **c**), the word that best conveys Mr. Collins's intense hatred of tomatoes is *detested*.

14. **d. hilarious.** The most important clue here is that the audience was "practically rolling on the ground with laughter." The movie must be extremely funny for the audience to have this sort of reaction, and, while all of the answer choices are synonyms for *funny*, the only one that means *extremely* funny is *hilarious* (choice **d**).

15. **c. hospitality.** All four choices describe different types of kindness. *Unselfishness* (choice **a**) can be ruled out, because *unselfishness* has the same basic meaning as the adjective *generous*. *Charity* (choice **d**) is a kindness that is generally shown to those less fortunate than oneself; because nothing in the context indicates that this is the relationship between the grandparents and the writer, this choice can be discounted. Left with a choice between *politeness* (choice **b**) and *hospitality* (choice **c**), the choice that best describes the kindness of welcoming someone into your home is choice **c**, *hospitality*.

GAME TIME: CONNOTATION CROSS-OUT SOLUTION

1. extremely poor: **destitute**
2. with emphasis: **emphatic**
3. drive: **ambition**
4. lively: **spirited**
5. weakened by old age; feeble: **decrepit**
6. practicing smart economic management: **thrifty**
7. state definitively: **proclaim**
8. fascinating: **engrossing**

Quote: *My fellow Americans: Ask not what your country can do for you—ask what you can do for your country.*

Parlez-Vous Français?
Words from Foreign Languages

The title of this chapter, "Parlez-Vous Français?" means, "Do you speak French?" The answer might surprise you! The truth is, you *do* speak some French, even though you may not know it. You speak French, German, Spanish, Italian, Arabic, Greek, and Latin on a regular basis, because words from all of these languages are frequently used in English. For example, have you said you were experiencing "déjà vu"? *Déjà vu* is a French phrase meaning "already seen," and it is used to describe the feeling of having been in the same situation once before. There is no English phrase that means the same thing as déjà vu, so we have taken the entire phrase and incorporated it into our language.

As you learned in Chapter 1, the English language is composed of words from a wide variety of sources. Word roots, suffixes, and prefixes often come from Greek and Latin sources. As the English language developed, we started to take these original languages and combine them to form the words that are the basis of our everyday conversation.

In some cases, we left the words exactly the way they were in their original languages. Instead of developing new words that were the English equivalents of these foreign words, we continued to use the words themselves. Although we use words from many different languages, the most common sources for new English words are French, German, Italian, and Spanish.

PRACTICE LAP

Choose the foreign word that is described by each definition.

1. Which of the following is a Spanish word meaning "big party"?
    a. piñata
    b. gaucho
    c. adobe
    d. fiesta

2. Which of the following is an Italian word that describes something that has gone horribly wrong?
    a. villa
    b. fiasco
    c. piazza
    d. mozzarella

3. Which of the following is a French word meaning "expert"?
    a. connoisseur
    b. blasé
    c. denouement
    d. naïve

4. Which of the following is a French word meaning an "overused expression"?
    a. trite
    b. cliché
    c. ennui
    d. liaison

5. Which of the following is a German word meaning "the grade before first grade"?
    a. kindergarten
    b. école
    c. preschool
    d. escuela

You'll find the answers at the end of the chapter.

FUEL FOR THOUGHT

AMERICA IS OFTEN described as a "melting pot," meaning it's a place where people from many different cultures can come and join as one culture. Recently, many people have begun to question whether this is an appropriate phrase to describe what actually happens when people from different cultures move to America.

Instead of thinking of America as a melting pot, some people prefer to think of it as a salad bowl. In a melting pot, many different foods blend together to create one taste. In a salad bowl, however, each ingredient of the salad contributes to the taste of the salad, yet each keeps its individual taste.

The salad bowl analogy is, perhaps, a more appropriate way to describe our great country. Americans do not all have one culture. The way people live in New York City is very different from the way people live in Alaska. As Americans, we have the freedom to practice our own religions, dress however we want to, and speak whatever language we are comfortable speaking. People who move here from foreign countries have the freedom to keep whatever aspects of their cultures they would like to keep, and to pass their culture on to their fellow countrymen and women.

Many new words come into our language from these sources. The ability to change and adapt to new cultures is what makes America unlike any other country in the world.

WHY DO WE NEED FOREIGN WORDS?

Foreign words are often adopted into English because there are no English words that have the same meaning. For example, take the French word *naïve*. To be naïve is to have a simple, childlike view of something. There is no English word that expresses the same concept as naïve. You might say, "It is *naïve* of Jennifer to think that she can finish all of her homework before the baseball game." The connotation is slightly negative, but not as negative as a word like *stupid* or *ignorant*. It is often used to imply that things are slightly more complex than someone might imagine.

Other foreign words are used simply for variety. The word *ciao* is an Italian greeting that means both *hello* and *goodbye*. Although we could easily say *hello* or *goodbye* to people, sometimes people use the word *ciao* just to say something different.

RECOGNIZING FOREIGN WORDS

Some foreign words have become so common to the English language that they no longer stand out as being from foreign sources. *Hamburger*, for instance, was a word created by German immigrants, yet it is used so often that it is not thought of as a German word. On the other hand, a word like *kaput*, a German word meaning "broken," still stands out as being from a foreign culture.

Foreign words often stand out because of the way they are pronounced. The word *kaput*, for example, is pronounced *ka-puut*. If this word had originated in English, it would most likely be pronounced *ka-put*.

When a word does not obey standard English rules of pronunciation, chances are good that word will come from a foreign language. The word *debut*, for instance, is a French word meaning "first performance." It is pronounced *de-byoo*. If it were originally an English word, it would probably be pronounced *de-butt*.

Foreign languages have their own looks and patterns of pronunciation that can be learned. German words often have hard *g* or *k* sounds. There will often be long combinations of consonants, including the combination *sch*. *Schnauzer* (a type of dog) is a German word, as is *kitsch* (gaudy trash). French words, on the other hand, often have soft consonant and vowel sounds. *Déjà vu*, for example, is pronounced *de-szah voo*. Italian words often end in *o* or *a*, as in *bravo* (a cry of approval) and *a cappella* (singing without musical accompaniment). Spanish words are often short words that end in vowels, like *siesta* (a midday nap) or *macho* (manly).

French words and phrases can often be recognized because they use **diacritical marks**. Diacritical marks are accent marks that tell you how a letter is pronounced, like the *é* in *cliché* or the *ï* in *naïve*. Words that originated in English do not use diacritical marks.

PRACTICE LAP

Read each word or phrase and determine which language the word or phrase comes from.

6. *vis-à-vis* (veez-ah-vee) *adj.* face to face
   a. German
   b. French
   c. Spanish
   d. Italian

7. *incognito* (in-kog-nee-toh) *adj.* or *adv.* with one's identity concealed
   a. German
   b. French
   c. Spanish
   d. Italian

8. *blasé* (blah-zay) *adj.* uninterested; bored
   a. German
   b. French
   c. Spanish
   d. Italian

9. *rodeo* (roh-dee-oh) *n.* a public exhibition of cowboy or cowgirl skills
   a. German
   b. French
   c. Spanish
   d. Italian

10. *angst* (ankst) *n.* a feeling of dread
   a. German
   b. French
   c. Spanish
   d. Italian

Check your answers on page 139.

FOREIGN PHRASES

Sometimes, instead of taking single words, we borrow entire phrases from other cultures. These phrases are used as though they were single words. For example, the French phrase *hors d'oeuvres* is used to mean "appetizers" in English. The French phrase is composed of three different words: *hors* (outside), *de* (of), and *oeuvres* (a body of work). In English, the phrase is used as single noun.

More often than not, if an entire phrase comes from a foreign language, it will have a French origin. When we use phrases from languages besides French, we tend to use them in the exact way they are used in their original language. For instance, we might say *hasta la vista* instead of goodbye. The phrase is used in the original Spanish in exactly the same way. Some people say *danke schoen* instead of thank you. *Danke schoen* means "thank you" in German, its language of origin.

A wide variety of French phrases have worked their way into everyday usage. You can order pie *a la mode*, which means "with ice cream." If you wish someone a *bon voyage*, you are telling that person to have a good trip. A *cul-de-sac* is the end of a street, and a *faux pas* is a mistake. These and many other French phrases help give our language color and variety.

INSIDE TRACK

ALTHOUGH THE WORDS in this chapter have foreign origins, it is useful to remember that French, Italian, German, Spanish, and English all share common roots in Latin and Greek. Latin and Greek suffixes, prefixes, and roots can often be recognized in foreign words. These suffixes, prefixes, and roots can help you determine the meanings of words that you do not recognize. For example, the French word *malaise* means "a feeling of uneasiness." In this word, you can see the prefix *mal-*, meaning "bad, evil, or wrong."

PRACTICE LAP

Read each sentence. Use context clues to determine the meaning of each foreign word or phrase.

11. When my neighbor Luigi and I were younger, we were almost always together; to this day, he remains my closest *amigo*.
    Amigo means
    a. brother.
    b. house.
    c. friend.
    d. victim.

12. My father and I had a secret *rendezvous* to discuss plans for my mother's birthday party.
    Rendezvous means
    a. decision.
    b. dinner.
    c. meeting.
    d. committee.

13. The *spiel* in the advertisement claimed that the laundry detergent cleaned better than any other detergent on the market.
    Spiel is
    a. language used to sell something.
    b. a picture of a product.
    c. a type of laundry detergent.
    d. beautiful writing.

14. My grandmother handed me $30 and gave me *carte blanche* to buy anything I wanted with it.
    Carte blanche is
    a. total power.
    b. a warning.
    c. unlimited funds.
    d. a bad idea.

15. Isabella claimed that she enjoyed her meal, but her sour expression told me her reaction was just a *façade*.

A *façade* is a

a. silly mistake.

b. humorous story.

c. look of excitement.

d. false appearance.

Check your answers on pages 139–140.

CROSSING THE FINISH LINE

In this chapter, we learned that there are many foreign language words and phrases used in the English language. The most common sources for new English words are French, German, Italian, and Spanish.

Foreign words are often adopted into English because there are no English words that have the same meaning. Other times, foreign words are used for variety.

Foreign words can be recognized by the way they are pronounced. Foreign languages have their own looks and patterns of pronunciation that can be learned and recognized. French words and phrases can often be recognized because of their diacritical marks.

The French language has given us many phrases that we use regularly. With all foreign words, you can use suffixes, prefixes, and roots as clues to understanding the meaning of the words.

CHAPTER 8 WORD LIST

a cappella (ˈah kă·ˈpel·ă) *adj.* without musical accompaniment

a la mode (ah lah mohd) *adj.* with ice cream; literally "in the fashion"

adobe (ă·ˈdoh·bee) *n.* clay house

amigo (ă·ˈmee·goh) *n.* friend

analogy (ăn·ˈal·ŏ·jee) *n.* similarity between like features of two different things

angst (ankst) *n.* a feeling of dread

blasé (blah·ˈzay) *adj.* bored with life; difficult to impress bon voyage ('bahn voi·'aj) *int.* have a good trip

bravo ('bră·voh) *int.* well done

carte blanche (kahrt blahnsh) *n.* unconditional authority

ciao (chow) *int.* hello or goodbye

cliché (klee·'shay) *n.* a phrase or idea that has been repeated so often as to lose effectiveness

connoisseur (kon·oh·'sŭr) *n.* expert; someone who knows a large amount about a certain subject

cul·de·sac ('kul·dĭ·sak) *n.* the end of a road

debut (day·'bŭ) *n.* premier performance

déjà vu ('day·zhah 'voo) *n.* the feeling that one has been in a situation before

denouement ('day·noo·mon) *n.* the final resolution of a plot in a work of drama or fiction

diacritical marks (dī·ă·'krit·ĭ·kĕl 'mărks) *n.* linguistic marks that give information about how words are pronounced

ennui (on·'wee) *n.* boredom

façade (fă·'sahd) *n.* false front

fiasco (fee·'as·ko) *n.* disastrous situation

fiesta (fee·'ĕs·tă) *n.* party

gaucho ('gow·choh) *n.* cowboy

hors d'oeuvres (ohr 'durvs) *n.* appetizers

incognito (in·kog·'nee·toh) *adj.* or *adv.* with one's identity concealed

kaput (kă·'puut) *adj.* broken

kitsch (kitsh) *n.* art or objects that are designed to appeal to people with undiscriminating taste

liaison (lee·'ay·zŏn) *n.* meeting

macho ('mah·choh) *adj.* manly

malaise (mă·'layz) *n.* feeling of mental discomfort

naïve (nī·'eev) *adj.* showing simplicity or a lack of experience

piazza (pee·'ă·ză) *n.* open square in the middle of a city or town

piñata (pin·'yah·tă) *n.* a papier.mâché-figure filled with candy and broken during parties

rendezvous ('ron·day·voo) *n.* secret meeting

rodeo ('roh·dee·oh) *n.* a public exhibition of cowboy or cowgirl skills

schnauzer ('shnow·zur) *n.* type of dog

siesta (see·'ĕs·tă) *n.* afternoon nap

spiel (shpeel) *n.* talk given for the purposing of luring an audience or sell-
   ing a product

trite (trīt) *adj.* lacking in effectiveness

villa ('vee·lah) *n.* a country estate

vis·à·vis ('veez·ah·vee) *adj.* face to face

GAME TIME: LETTER FILL-IN

Find the foreign word from the Chapter 8 Word List on pages 135–136 that
fits each definition. When you're done, put the letters in their corresponding
boxes to read a quote by comedian Groucho Marx.

1. *n.* expert; someone who knows a large amount about a certain subject:

— — — — — — — — — — —
   42   23 1 32 50   7   60

2. *intj.* have a good trip:

— — —   — — — — — —
26 59   17   14 13 33

3. *n.* a public exhibition of cowboy or cowgirl skills:

— — — — —
56   54 61 12

4. *adj.* broken:

— — — — —
18 62   2

5. *n.* meeting:

— — — — — — —
  5   36 20 52 37

6. *n.* false front:

$\underline{\quad}$ $\underline{\quad}$ $\underline{\quad}$ $\underline{\quad}$ $\underline{\quad}$ $\underline{\quad}$
30   55   11   41

7. *n.* disastrous situation:

$\underline{\quad}$ $\underline{\quad}$ $\underline{\quad}$ $\underline{\quad}$ $\underline{\quad}$ $\underline{\quad}$
9   19   22   24   16

8. *n.* art or objects that are designed to appeal to people with undiscriminating tastes:

$\underline{\quad}$ $\underline{\quad}$ $\underline{\quad}$ $\underline{\quad}$ $\underline{\quad}$ $\underline{\quad}$
57   48   29

9. *n.* premier performance:

$\underline{\quad}$ $\underline{\quad}$ $\underline{\quad}$ $\underline{\quad}$ $\underline{\quad}$
6   27   49

10. *n.* party:

$\underline{\quad}$ $\underline{\quad}$ $\underline{\quad}$ $\underline{\quad}$ $\underline{\quad}$
43   39   28   3

11. *n.* feeling of dread:

$\underline{\quad}$ $\underline{\quad}$ $\underline{\quad}$ $\underline{\quad}$ $\underline{\quad}$
44   47   58

12. *n.* clay house:

$\underline{\quad}$ $\underline{\quad}$ $\underline{\quad}$ $\underline{\quad}$ $\underline{\quad}$
45   53   15

13. *n.* secret meeting:

— — — — — — — — — —
31   63   46   38

14. *n.* the final resolution of a plot in a work of drama or fiction:

— — — — — — — — —
40   34 8   21   51

15. *n.* the end of the road:

— — — - — — - — — —
        35   4 10

Quote

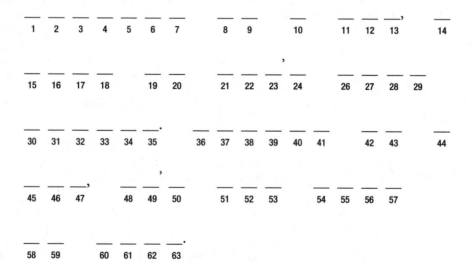

ANSWERS

1. **d. fiesta.** A *fiesta* is a festive celebration. Sample sentence: Consuela's parents are throwing her a big *fiesta* for her birthday.
2. **b. fiasco.** A *fiasco* is something that has gone terribly wrong. Sample sentence: When I heard that the band couldn't make it to the party, I was worried that it was going to be a major *fiasco*.

3. a. connoisseur. A *connoisseur* is someone who knows a lot about a subject. Sample sentence: Frederick is a cheese *connoisseur*; he has tried kinds of cheeses that I've never even heard of!

4. b. cliché. A *cliché* is an expression that is overused, like "crazy like a fox." Sample sentence: I didn't like Edwin's story because I felt that he used too many *clichés*.

5. a. kindergarten. *Kindergarten* is the grade before first grade. It was originally a German word that has become regularly used in English. Sample sentence: Tilly's little sister is starting *kindergarten* in the fall.

6. b. French. The diacritical marks give this word away. Also, although we have taken many words from foreign languages, the majority of foreign phrases used in English actually come from French.

7. d. Italian. *Incognito* is an Italian word. The final *o* is sometimes a clue that a word comes from Italian.

8. b. French. Again, the main clue in this word is the diacritical mark. Also notice the pronunciation—the letter *s* is sometimes pronounced like a *z* in French words.

9. c. Spanish. *Rodeo* is a short word with three vowel sounds, which makes it likely that it is a Spanish word. Although not all Spanish words follow these rules, it is a common trait of some Spanish words borrowed into English.

10. a. German. Notice the four consonants at the end of the word. When there are several consonants placed next to each other, chances are strong the word will be German in origin.

11. c. friend. *Amigo* is Spanish for "friend." Choice **b** can be ruled out, as a person could not be described as a *house*. *Victim* (choice **d**) does not make much sense considering the context of the sentence. Because you know that Luigi is the writer's next-door neighbor, he is most likely not the writer's brother (choice **a**), so the only remaining choice is **c**, *friend*.

12. c. meeting. *Rendezvous* is a French word meaning "meeting." A *committee* (choice **d**) is generally composed of more than two people, so that option can be discounted. *Decision* (choice **a**) does not make much sense in the context of the sentence. While they could have discussed these plans over dinner (choice **b**), the more likely choice is **c**, *meeting*.

13. a. language used to sell something. *Spiel* is a German word. A picture of a product (choice **b**) could not make a claim, so this option can be discounted. Although the sentence is about laundry detergent, choice **c** does not work in context. The writing in the ad could be *beautiful* (choice **d**), but it is more likely that the *spiel* in the ad is the language used to sell the product.

14. **a. total power.** *Carte blanche* is a French phrase, meaning literally "blank check." The writer's grandmother did not give her a warning, so choice **b** is incorrect. If you know the writer received $30, then you can't say she had unlimited funds, so choice **c** is not the best option. While some might say it's a *bad idea* (choice **d**) to go around handing money out, the most likely choice based on context is choice **a**, *total power*.

15. **d. false appearance.** The context tells you that Isabella was not telling the truth about how much she enjoyed the meal. Based on this information, you can rule out *silly mistake* (choice **a**), *humorous story* (choice **b**), and *look of excitement* (choice **c**).

GAME TIME: LETTER FILL-IN SOLUTION

1. *n.* expert; someone who knows a large amount about a certain subject:

c   o   n   n   o   i   s   s   e   u   r
     42   23   1   32 50   7   60

2. *intj.* have a good trip:

b   o   n   v   o   y   a   g   e
26 59   17   14 13 33

3. *n.* a public exhibition of cowboy or cowgirl skills:

r   o   d   e   o
56   54 61 12

4. *adj.* broken:

k   a   p   u   t
18 62   2

5. *n.* meeting:

$$\underline{l}\ \underline{i}\ \underline{a}\ \underline{i}\ \underline{s}\ \underline{o}\ \underline{n}$$
$$536\ \ 20\ \ 52\ \ 37$$

6. *n.* false front:

$$\underline{f}\ \underline{a}\ \underline{ç}\ \underline{a}\ \underline{d}\ \underline{e}$$
$$3055\ \ 11\ \ 41$$

7. *n.* disastrous situation:

$$\underline{f}\ \underline{i}\ \underline{a}\ \underline{s}\ \underline{c}\ \underline{o}$$
$$9\ \ 19\ \ 22\ \ 2416$$

8. *n.* art or objects that are designed to appeal to people with undiscriminating tastes:

$$\underline{k}\ \underline{i}\ \underline{t}\ \underline{s}\ \underline{c}\ \underline{h}$$
$$57\ \ 48\ \ 29$$

9. *n.* premier performance:

$$\underline{d}\ \underline{e}\ \underline{b}\ \underline{u}\ \underline{t}$$
$$6\ \ 2749$$

10. *n.* party:

$$\underline{f}\ \underline{i}\ \underline{e}\ \underline{s}\ \underline{t}\ \underline{a}$$
$$43\ \ 3928\ \ 3$$

11. *n.* feeling of dread:

$$\underline{a}\ \underline{n}\ \underline{g}\ \underline{s}\ \underline{t}$$
$$444758$$

12. *n.* clay house:

<u>a</u>   <u>d</u>   <u>o</u>   <u>b</u>   <u>e</u>
     45   53   15

13. *n.* secret meeting:

<u>r</u>   <u>e</u>   <u>n</u>   <u>d</u>   <u>e</u>   <u>z</u>   <u>v</u>   <u>o</u>   <u>u</u>   <u>s</u>
31   63   46   38

14. *n.* the final resolution of a plot in a work of drama or fiction:

<u>d</u>   <u>e</u>   <u>n</u>   <u>o</u>   <u>u</u>   <u>m</u>   <u>e</u>   <u>n</u>   <u>t</u>
40   34   8   21   51

15. *n.* the end of the road:

<u>c</u>   <u>u</u>   <u>l</u>   -   <u>d</u>   <u>e</u>   -   <u>s</u>   <u>a</u>   <u>c</u>
         35   4   10

Quote

<u>O</u>   <u>u</u>   <u>t</u>   <u>s</u>   <u>i</u>   <u>d</u>   <u>e</u>   <u>o</u>   <u>f</u>   <u>a</u>   <u>d</u>   <u>o</u>   <u>g</u>,   <u>a</u>
1 2 3 4 5 6 7   8 9   10   11 12 13   14

<u>b</u>   <u>o</u>   <u>o</u>   <u>k</u>   <u>i</u>   <u>s</u>   <u>m</u>   <u>a</u>   <u>n</u>'   <u>s</u>   <u>b</u>   <u>e</u>   <u>s</u>   <u>t</u>
15 16 17 18 19 20 21 22 23 24 26 27 28 29

<u>f</u>   <u>r</u>   <u>i</u>   <u>e</u>   <u>n</u>   <u>d</u>.   <u>I</u>   <u>n</u>   <u>s</u>   <u>i</u>   <u>d</u>   <u>e</u>   <u>o</u>   <u>f</u>   <u>a</u>
30 31 32 33 34 35 36 37 38 39 40 41 42 43 44

<u>d</u>   <u>o</u>   <u>g</u>,   <u>i</u>   <u>t</u>'   <u>s</u>   <u>t</u>   <u>o</u>   <u>o</u>   <u>d</u>   <u>a</u>   <u>r</u>   <u>k</u>
45 46 47 48 49 50 51 52 53 54 55 56 57

<u>t</u>   <u>o</u>   <u>r</u>   <u>e</u>   <u>a</u>   <u>d</u>.
58 59 60 61 62 63

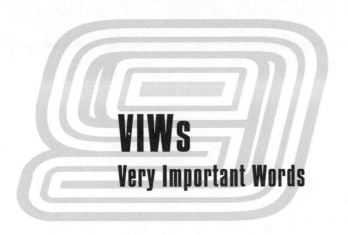

VIWs
Very Important Words

L **et's set up** a *hypothetical* situation. Your teacher asks you to write an essay, but you don't have a *thesis* you would like to prove. So, you go to the library and leaf through a number of *tomes* to find something to write about. Finally, you come across a book on popular sports of *antiquity*. You decide your paper will be an *inquiry* into the difference between modern sports and sports of *bygone* eras. Unfortunately, your teacher fails to grasp the *academic* merit of your paper. "This is simply not up to *caliber*," he tells you, after *evaluating* your work.

The italicized words in the previous paragraph are all words that you may not know. Although they may seem complex, these words are all words that you may come across in your daily life. We'll call these words VIWs (very important words), because they are words that may not be familiar, but that everyone should know. By learning the meanings of these VIWs, you can start to read and write at higher grade levels. Your teachers and friends will be wowed by your impressive vocabulary, and this will help you avoid the painful situation described in the previous paragraph.

PRACTICE LAP

Read the first paragraph of this chapter again. Using the knowledge you've gained throughout the book, try to choose the best definition of the italicized word in each question.

1. A *hypothetical* situation is a situation that is
   a. unbelievable.
   b. humorous.
   c. imagined.
   d. exciting.

2. A *thesis* is
   a. an impossible situation.
   b. a well-written paper.
   c. a subject for an essay.
   d. an undeveloped idea.

3. A *tome* is
   a. a large book.
   b. a library table.
   c. a modern magazine.
   d. an encyclopedia.

4. Something that is of *antiquity* is
   a. dull.
   b. expensive.
   c. ancient.
   d. quaint.

5. An *inquiry* is
   a. an investigation.
   b. a problem.
   c. a result.
   d. a thought.

6. *Bygone* means
   a. foreign.
   b. days.
   c. simple.
   d. past.

7. Something that lacks *academic* merit is
    a. hard to explain.
    b. not worth studying.
    c. full of lies.
    d. easy to understand.

8. Something that is not up to *caliber* does not
    a. meet the requirements.
    b. need any further explanation.
    c. make any sense.
    d. look very pretty.

9. To *evaluate* is to
    a. forget immediately.
    b. look at quickly.
    c. consider carefully.
    d. perform poorly.

You'll find the answers at the end of the chapter.

VIWS RELATED TO SCHOOL

School is where you spend a large share of your time. Following is a list of important words related to school. Some of these words you may know already; others may not be so familiar. All of them are VIWs that you will someday see often.

administration (ad·min·i·′stray·shun) *n.* management; the principal, superintendent, school board members, and others who run a school or school system. *Before my teacher could take us on a field trip, she had to clear it with the administration.*

analyze (′an·ul·īz) *v.* to examine critically. *Today, we are going to analyze poetry.*

assessment (uh·′ses·mint) *n.* the act of determining something's worth; a standardized test. *Next week, Jao's class will begin practicing for the state assessments.*

comprehend (kom·pree·′hĕnd) *v.* to understand. *It is easier for me to comprehend algebra than geometry.*

criteria (krī·'teer·ee·uh) *n. pl.* (singular: criterion) standards by which a judgment is based; rules. *You must meet several criteria in order to enter the science fair.*

curriculum (kur·'ick·yoo·lum) *n.* the complete selection of courses offered by a school system. *Algebra II was offered as part of the curriculum at Mindy's school.*

data ('day·tuh) *n. pl.* (singular: datum) facts; items of information. *After we run our tests, we will take a close look at the data we've gathered.*

deduce (dee·'doos) *v.* to draw a conclusion from evidence. *Janelle deduced from the experiment results that she had added too much water to her mixture.*

extracurricular (eck·stră·kur·'ick·yoo·lur) *adj.* activities that take place outside of regular school hours. *Marcus is involved in many different extracurricular activities, including the soccer team and student council.*

facilitate (fu·'sil·u·tayt) *v.* to make easier. *The way our chairs are arranged in English class really facilitates discussion.*

lecturer (lek·'shur·ur) *n.* speaker. *We had a brilliant guest lecturer in art class today.*

parameter (pur·'am·uh·tur) *n.* limits. *Mr. Stevenson explained the parameters of the assignment.*

philosophy (fil·'ah·soh·fee) *n.* a set of ideas. *My philosophy is that standardized tests are not a useful learning tool.*

INSIDE TRACK

WHEN YOU LEARN one new word, the knowledge doesn't just stop there. For example, as you can see from the school VIWs list, the word *facilitate* means "to make easier." Based on this information, what do you think the word *facile* means?

a. stupid

b. easily done

c. swift

d. more difficult

That's right, the correct answer is choice **b**, *easily done*. Always keep in mind: Every word you learn can be used as a key to unlock meaning in other unfamiliar words.

VIWS RELATED TO WORK

Why do we spend so much time in school, anyway? Answer: to prepare ourselves for the inevitable day when we must spend even more time at work. Get a leg up on the competition by learning this group of work-related VIWs.

ascertain (a·sur·ʹtayn) *v.* to find out. *My company took a survey to ascertain the level of demand for our new product.*

configure (kun·ʹfig·yur) *v.* to set up. *Configure your new password after you log on to the corporate website.*

corporation (kor·pur·ʹa·shun) *n.* a company. *Wal-Mart is one of the most successful corporations in the world.*

department (dee·ʹpärt·mĕnt) *n.* a division within a company. *I work in the accounting department.*

differentiate (dif·ur·ʹĕn·shee·ayt) *v.* to distinguish between. *It's hard for me to differentiate between the two new ad campaigns; they both seem similar.*

implement (im·ʹpluh·mĕnt) *v.* to put into effect. *Sheila was asked to implement some changes in the way she signs her e-mails.*

institute (ʹin·stu·toot) *v.* to establish. *The boss decided to institute a casual dress policy for Fridays.*

interview (ʹin·tur·vyoo) *n.* a formal meeting set up when attempting to be hired for a new job. *I have an interview with the manager of the bank on Friday to work as a teller.*

manufacture (man·yoo·ʹfak·shur) *v.* to make. *My company manufactures a variety of different food products.*

policy (ʹpahl·i·see) *n.* a course of action; rule. *Our policy is to treat customers with respect.*

portfolio (pohrt·ʹfoh·lee·oh) *n.* a collection of pieces of personal work shown when interviewing for a job. *I put together a portfolio of my best articles from the school newspaper.*

procedure (pro·ʹseed·yur) *n.* a way of doing something. *Your welcome package will explain all of our company's policies and procedures.*

product (ʹprah·dukt) *n.* a thing being produced or manufactured. *The company I work for manufactures beauty products, and we always get to take home free samples.*

resume ('rĕz·u·may) *n.* a printed overview of one's previous job experience. *My career counselor said that it's best to keep your resume to a single sheet of paper.*

salary ('sal·ur·ee) *n.* the amount a job pays. *The starting salary at my company is $20,000 per year.*

INSIDE TRACK

IN MOST CASES, the words on the VIW lists aren't strictly related to the categories in which they appear. For instance, even though *institute* is a common word in the professional world, it can be used to describe anything that is being established. You can *institute* a new rule that you're going to eat only vanilla ice cream, or you can *institute* a newspaper at your school. You can find most of the words on these lists used in a wide variety of situations, which is what turns them from just ordinary words into very important words. Now that you know these words, keep an eye out for them; you might be surprised at how common many of them are.

LITERATURE-RELATED VIWS

Following is a list of useful words that are used when discussing literature. These words often appear on standardized tests.

ambiguous (am·'big·yoo·us) *adj.* having several different possible meanings. *The writer purposely made the ending of the book ambiguous so that people could make up their own minds about what happened.*

clarify ('klair·i·fy) *v.* to make clear. *Can you clarify the difference between the two poems?*

climax ('klī·maks) *n.* the decisive moment in a story. *At the climax of* The Wizard of Oz, *Dorothy must choose between staying with her new friends and returning to Kansas.*

emphasize ('ĕm·fă·sīz) *v.* to single out as important. *This article emphasizes the importance of eating a balanced diet.*

exposition (ĕks·poh·'zi·shun) *n.* the part of the story that sets up the plot. *Important details about Alice's character in* Alice in Wonderland *are laid out in the exposition at the beginning of the book.*

figurative ('fig·yur·it·iv) *adj.* not literal. *Poetry often uses figurative language to convey feelings that are difficult to put into words.*

hyperbole (hī·'pur·buh·lee) *n.* intentional exaggeration. *The author used hyperbole when he said the pig was "as big as a house."*

interpret (in·'tur·prĕt) *v.* to explain the meaning of. *How would you interpret the author's use of figurative language?*

literal ('li·tur·ul) *adj.* the actual meaning. *The literal translation of the word* bonjour *is "good day."*

plot ('plaht) *n.* the course of events in a story. *This book has a great plot; I couldn't wait to read what was going to happen next.*

setting ('sĕt·ing) *n.* the environment in which a story takes place. *The setting of* Gone with the Wind *is a plantation during the Civil War.*

stanza ('stan·zuh) *n.* a group of lines in a poem. *This poem is composed of three stanzas with four lines in each stanza.*

summarize ('sum·ur·īz) *v.* to highlight the most important details. *Try to summarize the story in 50 words or less.*

theme ('theem) *n.* the main idea of a story. *The theme of this book is "never give up."*

tone ('tohn) *n.* the feeling of a story. *Most of my favorite films have a humorous tone.*

FUEL FOR THOUGHT

THE TAKING OF standardized tests has become a very common occurrence in American classrooms. These tests are called standardized tests because they're based on state *standards*, which are descriptions of the concepts that students should learn in each grade. Student scores on standardized tests are very important for school systems. If a school system does well on standardized tests, it gets more money from the government to pay for school supplies, interesting classes, extracurricular activities, and teacher salaries.

Although school standards differ from state to state, there are common elements that are often seen on standardized tests. Most state English tests feature a mixture of literature questions based on reading selections and stand-alone questions about vocabulary words and grammar. The structure of these questions is often very similar. For instance, one common thing that students are asked to do is to make predictions about what will happen based on information in a story. This standard requires students to pay attention to clues in a story and predict the outcome. More often than not, if you see the phrase *continue to* in one of the answer choices, this will be the correct answer.

Standardized tests have their own logic that can be understood by paying careful attention. In many ways, they are like a video game, where you must figure out the rules to solve the puzzles. As you take standardized tests, pay close attention to the way items are worded. If you can figure out the logic behind a test question, you can often figure out the correct answer based on clues in the question and answer choices.

PRACTICE LAP

Read each sentence and choose the VIW that best fits in the blank.

10. Richard was sick from school today, and he asked me to _____ our homework assignment for him.
    a. implement
    b. facilitate
    c. summarize
    d. comprehend

11. The sales _____ at my company is having a competition to see who can make the most sales in a week.
    a. department
    b. corporation
    c. administration
    d. lecturer

12. This poem means exactly what it says; it is very _____.
   a. literal
   b. extracurricular
   c. figurative
   d. ambiguous

13. The test directions were a little confusing, so I asked my teacher to _____ them for me.
   a. ascertain
   b. configure
   c. clarify
   d. manufacture

14. The college interviewer asked me to bring in a(n) _____ to show her my artwork.
   a. resume
   b. portfolio
   c. salary
   d. assessment

15. My school library has a _____ of charging five cents for every day a book is late.
   a. policy
   b. parameter
   c. curriculum
   d. philosophy

16. The _____ of this story is that money can't buy happiness.
   a. setting
   b. plot
   c. tone
   d. theme

17. The sentence context helped me _____ the meaning of the word.
    a. emphasize
    b. deduce
    c. evaluate
    d. differentiate

18. I'm starting a company to _____ my own greeting cards.
    a. evaluate
    b. interpret
    c. manufacture
    d. facilitate

Check your answers on page 157.

CROSSING THE FINISH LINE

In this chapter, we learned about VIWs, difficult words that are useful to know. VIWs are helpful for reading and writing at higher grade levels. We learned that learning these important words can help us understand the meaning of other words. VIWs are not strictly related to their categories; the words can be used in a variety of situations.

We also learned that standardized test questions have their own logic. To find the correct answer on standardized tests, it is helpful to pay attention to the questions and answer choices. The questions and answer choices contain valuable clues that can help you to determine the correct answer.

GAME TIME: BOX SHIFT

Unscramble the letters in the boxes that follow to match each definition from the Chapter 9 Word List on pages 155–156. Enter the unscrambled word in the empty boxes. Each scrambled word has a number of extra letters. Enter these extra letters into the bonus boxes. When you are all done, the letters in the bonus boxes will unscramble to spell one of the longest words in the English language, which was mentioned in an earlier chapter.

1. *v.* to establish

¹ | T | N | T | N | S | U | I | T | E | L | I |

2. *n.* a collection of pieces of creative work

² | O | R | O | L | T | O | F | I | I | N | P |

3. *v.* to set up

³ | N | R | G | D | C | F | O | E | U | E | I |

4. *n.* intentional exaggeration

⁴ | H | E | B | P | T | Y | R | O | A | E | L |

5. *v.* to find out

⁵ | S | E | C | I | N | I | R | I | T | A | A |

6. *v.* to single out as important

⁶ | P | E | A | H | E | M | I | A | Z | S | A |

7. *n.* the act of determining someone's worth; a standardized test

⁷ | S | A | S | M | T | S | I | S | E | N | E |

8. *v.* to set up

⁸ | F | G | I | C | S | R | M | N | U | E | O |

9. *n.* a way of doing something

⁹ | D | P | R | E | E | U | S | C | R | R | O |

10. *v.* to make easier

¹⁰ | A | I | T | T | E | N | C | A | I | L | F | □

11. *v.* to put into effect

¹¹ | E | M | N | M | I | M | P | T | L | T | E | □ □

12. *n.* the part of the story that sets up the plot

¹² | O | I | E | S | X | T | O | I | P | I | N | □

13. *n.* a set of ideas

¹³ | S | O | I | P | O | H | P | H | S | Y | L | □

14. *n.* theory

¹⁴ | P | H | S | Y | E | H | I | T | S | T | O | □

15. *n.* the quality of being ancient

¹⁵ | U | T | E | A | I | Q | T | N | I | A | Y | □ □

16. *n. pl.* standards by which a judgment is based; rules

¹⁶ | E | H | C | R | T | B | R | I | I | I | A | □ □ □

One of the longest words in the English language:

_ _

CHAPTER 9 WORD LIST

academic (a·kuh·ˈdĕm·ik) *adj.* related to school

administration (ad·min·i·ˈstray·shun) *n.* management; the principal, superintendent, school board members, and others who run a school or school system

ambiguous (am·ˈbig·yoo·us) *adj.* having several different possible meanings

analyze (ˈan·ul·īz) *v.* to examine critically

antiquity (an·ˈtik·kwuh·tee) *n.* the quality of being ancient

ascertain (a·sur·ˈtayn) *v.* to find out

assessment (uh·ˈses·mint) *n.* the act of determining something's worth; a standardized test

bygone (ˈbī·gawn) *adj.* past

caliber (ˈkal·i·bur) *n.* a level of strength or quality

clarify (ˈklair·i·fy) *v.* to make clear

climax (ˈklī·maks) *n.* the decisive moment in a story

comprehend (kom·pree·ˈhĕnd) *v.* to understand

configure (kun·ˈfig·yur) *v.* to set up

corporation (kor·pur·ˈa·shun) *n.* a company

criteria (krī·ˈteer·ee·uh) *n. pl.* (singular: criterion) standards by which a judgment is based; rules

curriculum (kur·ˈick·yoo·lum) *n.* the complete selection of courses offered by a school system

data (ˈday·tuh) *n. pl.* (singular: datum) facts; items of information

deduce (dee·ˈdoos) *v.* to draw a conclusion from evidence

department (dee·ˈpărt·mĕnt) *n.* a division within a company

differentiate (dif·ur·ˈĕn·shee·ayt) *v.* to distinguish between

emphasize (ˈĕm·fă·sīz) *v.* to single out as important

evaluate (ee·ˈval·yoo·ayt) *v.* to determine the worth or value of

exposition (ĕks·poh·ˈzi·shun) *n.* the part of the story that sets up the plot

extracurricular (eck·stră·kur·ˈick·yoo·lur) *adj.* activities that take place outside of regular school hours

facilitate (fu·ˈsil·uh·tayt) *v.* to make easier

figurative (ˈfig·yur·it·iv) *adj.* not literal

hyperbole (hī·′pur·buh·lee) *n.* intentional exaggeration

hypothesis (hī·′pah·thuh·sis) *n.* theory

implement (im·*pluh*·měnt) *v.* to put into effect

inquiry (′in·kwur·ee) *n.* investigation

institute (′in·stu·toot) *v.* to establish

interpret (in·′tur·prĕt) *v.* to explain the meaning of

interview (′in·tur·vyoo) *n.* a formal meeting set up when attempting to be hired for a new job

lecturer (lek·′shur·ur) *n.* speaker

literal (′li·tur·ul) *adj.* the actual meaning

manufacture (man·yoo·′fak·shur) *v.* to make

parameter (pur·′am·uh·tur) *n.* limits

philosophy (fil·′ah·soh·fee) *n.* a set of ideas

plot (′plaht) *n.* the course of events in a story

policy (′pahl·i·see) *n.* a course of action; rule

portfolio (pohrt·′foh·lee·oh) *n.* a collection of pieces of personal work shown when interviewing for a job

procedure (pro·′seed·yur) *n.* a way of doing something

product (′prah·dukt) *n.* a thing being produced or manufactured

resume (′rĕz·u·may) *n.* a printed overview of one's previous job experience

salary (′sal·ur·ee) *n.* the amount a job pays

setting (′sĕt·ing) *n.* the environment in which a story takes place

stanza (′stan·zuh) *n.* a group of lines in a poem

summarize (′sum·ur·īz) *v.* to highlight the most important details

theme (′theem) *n.* the main idea of a story

thesis (′thee·sis) *n.* a subject for an essay

tome (′tohm) *n.* a book, especially a very heavy, large, or dense book

tone (′tohn) *n.* the feeling of a story

ANSWERS

1. **c. imagined.** A *hypothesis* is a theory. For instance, a scientist might make the *hypothesis* that a chimpanzee could learn how to say its name. The scientist imagines a possibility, and then runs tests to prove whether this *hypothesis* is correct. A *hypothetical* situation, therefore, is an imagined situation.

2. **c. subject for an essay.** Any essay that writes for or against an opinion must have a *thesis* statement. The writer generally places his or her thesis statement at the beginning of the essay, and then uses the rest of the paper to prove this thesis with examples. High school students spend a lot of time learning to write proper thesis statements; this is a word you will definitely use in the near future, if not already.

3. **a. large book.** *Tome* is often used to describe large, heavy books that can be difficult to understand. The word *tome* also conjures up images of old, dusty books that are not read very often. For instance, the library in a castle might be filled with *tomes*.

4. **c. ancient.** *Antiquity* is a form of the word *antique*. You probably already know that *antiques* are old pieces of furniture. If something is of *antiquity*, it is ancient.

5. **a. investigation.** You probably know that to *inquire* about something is to ask a question. *Inquiry* is a form of the word *inquire*, and it means "an investigation."

6. **d. past.** A *bygone* era is an era that has already "gone by"; that is, an era from the past.

7. **b. not worth studying.** *Academic* comes from the word *academy*, and it refers to things of a scholastic nature. If something lacks *academic* merit, it is not very scholarly, and therefore, it is not worth studying.

8. **a. meet the requirements.** *Caliber* is a level of strength or quality. Something that is *high caliber* is of excellent quality, while something that is *low caliber* is poorly made. If you are not up to caliber, you are not doing as well as you should or as well as others.

9. **c. consider carefully.** Every time you write a paper, your teacher *evaluates* your work and then decides what grade you deserve. It is implied that an *evaluation* will result in a decision. If you're not happy with the decision, you can sometimes ask for a *reevaluation*.

10. **c. summarize.** To *summarize* is to highlight the most important details. If your friend was sick from school, he might ask you for a brief explanation of the homework assignment, or a summary.

11. **a. department.** A *department* is a division within a company or corporation. The sentence describes a select division at a company; therefore, *department* is the best choice.

12. **a. literal.** When something has a *literal* meaning, it means exactly what it says. An *ambiguous* poem (choice **d**) would have a number of different interpretations, while a *figurative* poem (choice **c**) would not mean exactly what it says. A poem cannot be described as *extracurricular* (choice **b**); therefore, *literal* is the best answer choice.

13. **c. clarify.** According to the sentence, the test directions are difficult to understand. To *clarify* something is to make it easier to understand.

14. **b. portfolio.** A *portfolio* is a collection of personal work. If an interviewer wanted to see your creative work, he or she would ask you to bring in a portfolio.

15. **a. policy.** A *policy* is a rule. The sentence context implies that the school has a rule of charging five cents for late books; therefore, the best choice is choice **a**, *policy*.

16. **d. theme.** The *theme* of a story is the main idea. "Money can't buy happiness" describes an important idea in the story, so the best answer is choice **d**, *theme*.

17. **b. deduce.** The writer in the sample sentence used clues to find the meaning of the word. The choice that means to draw a conclusion from clues is choice **b**, *deduce*.

18. **c. manufacture.** The context of this sentence implies that the writer is planning to make his or her own greeting cards. The word that means "to make" is choice **c**, *manufacture*.

1. *v.* to establish

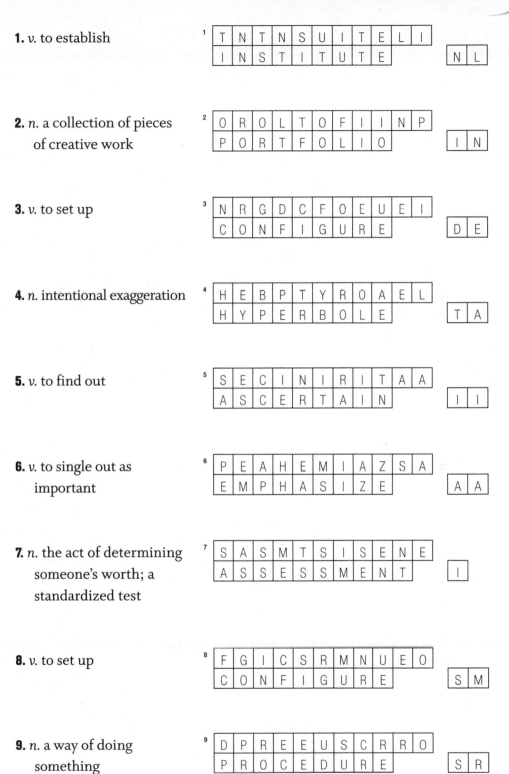

1	T	N	T	N	S	U	I	T	E	L	I
	I	N	S	T	I	T	U	T	E		

N	L

2. *n.* a collection of pieces of creative work

2	O	R	O	L	T	O	F	I	I	N	P
	P	O	R	T	F	O	L	I	O		

I	N

3. *v.* to set up

3	N	R	G	D	C	F	O	E	U	E	I
	C	O	N	F	I	G	U	R	E		

D	E

4. *n.* intentional exaggeration

4	H	E	B	P	T	Y	R	O	A	E	L
	H	Y	P	E	R	B	O	L	E		

T	A

5. *v.* to find out

5	S	E	C	I	N	I	R	I	T	A	A
	A	S	C	E	R	T	A	I	N		

I	I

6. *v.* to single out as important

6	P	E	A	H	E	M	I	A	Z	S	A
	E	M	P	H	A	S	I	Z	E		

A	A

7. *n.* the act of determining someone's worth; a standardized test

7	S	A	S	M	T	S	I	S	E	N	E
	A	S	S	E	S	S	M	E	N	T	

I

8. *v.* to set up

8	F	G	I	C	S	R	M	N	U	E	O
	C	O	N	F	I	G	U	R	E		

S	M

9. *n.* a way of doing something

9	D	P	R	E	E	U	S	C	R	R	O
	P	R	O	C	E	D	U	R	E		

S	R

10. *v.* to make easier

A	I	T	T	E	N	C	A	I	L	F

F	A	C	I	L	I	T	A	T	E

N

11. *v.* to put into effect

E	M	N	M	I	M	P	T	L	T	E

I	M	P	L	E	M	E	N	T

T	M

12. *n.* the part of the story that sets up the plot

O	I	E	S	X	T	O	I	P	I	N

E	X	P	O	S	I	T	I	O	N

I

13. *n.* a set of ideas

S	O	I	P	O	H	P	H	S	Y	L

P	H	I	L	O	S	O	P	H	Y

S

14. *n.* theory

P	H	S	Y	E	H	I	T	S	T	O

H	Y	P	O	T	H	E	S	I	S

T

15. *n.* the quality of being ancient

U	T	E	A	I	Q	T	N	I	A	Y

A	N	T	I	Q	U	I	T	Y

E	A

16. *n. pl.* standards by which a judgment is based; rules

E	H	C	R	T	B	R	I	I	I	A

C	R	I	T	E	R	I	A

I	B	H

One of the longest words in the English language:

ANTIDISESTABLISHMENTARIANISM

Posttest

The following posttest tests your knowledge of the skills you have learned in this book. Some of these words are taken from the vocabulary lists in the book. Others are new words that you should be able to figure out with the knowledge you've gained. After you're finished, check your answers on page 168 and see how you've done!

SENTENCE COMPLETION

The following exercise tests your knowledge of the vocabulary words that were featured in this book. Each sentence is followed by four answer choices. Your task is to choose the answer choice that best completes each sentence.

1. Rodrigo is a _____ musician; he can play the drums, piano, and guitar equally well.
   a. monotalented
   b. multitalented
   c. untalented
   d. semitalented

2. I was shocked to hear Louise give such a bitter _____ against the new math teacher.

    a. argument

    b. discussion

    c. diatribe

    d. talk

3. Although the fifth graders are mostly the same age, they _____ greatly in size.

    a. maintain

    b. disperse

    c. unify

    d. vary

4. My mom said that the plumber did not do a great job, but his work was _____.

    a. dysfunctional

    b. engrossing

    c. adequate

    d. calculating

5. I accidentally spilled water on my computer, which caused it to _____.

    a. multifunction

    b. functionate

    c. cofunction

    d. malfunction

6. Renee is so _____ that she refuses to loan me money, even though I really need it.

    a. stingy

    b. thrifty

    c. frugal

    d. inexpensive

7. Someone told Kyle the field trip was today, but he was _____; it's actually next week.
   a. overinformed
   b. monoinformed
   c. misinformed
   d. postinformed

8. The pop star had to be _____ in public so her fans wouldn't recognize her.
   a. incognito
   b. unmistakable
   c. hysterical
   d. blasé

9. The writing in that book is a little too _____ for me; I usually read books that are a lot more difficult.
   a. complex
   b. unimaginable
   c. scintillating
   d. simplistic

10. My teacher said he would accept any short story, as long as we stayed within the _____ of the assignment.
    a. policy
    b. department
    c. parameters
    d. results

11. The radio is _____ when played at such a low level.
    a. extensive
    b. inaudible
    c. captivating
    d. enhanced

12. Although the actress's _____ was in a forgettable film, her second performance was loved by critics everywhere.
    a. denouement
    b. façade
    c. debut
    d. ennui

13. Norton's _____ response told me he didn't really want to come over.
    a. regrettable
    b. unenthusiastic
    c. assured
    d. despicable

14. It is against the law to _____ the speed limit.
    a. exceed
    b. proceed
    c. precede
    d. recede

15. Antonio is a real slob; his clothes and toys are _____ thrown all over his room.
    a. significantly
    b. haphazardly
    c. unfortunately
    d. unintentionally

CHOOSE THE RIGHT WORD

Circle the italicized word that best completes the sentence.

16. The oil spill (*polluted/diluted*) the coastline, requiring a massive cleanup effort.

17. Give a nod of (*assent/ascent*) if you agree with me.

18. The human relations (*corporation/department*) is responsible for helping new employees learn more about the company.

19. The governor was (*deresponsive/unresponsive*) to the reporter's questions.

20. I realize the originality of this book is (*debatable/debatify*), but I still love it.

21. Dora hadn't read the book, so writing a paper on it was going to be a (*daunting/dauntless*) task.

22. You'll need a lot of (*ambition/willpower*) if you're planning on resisting my grandmother's delicious apple tarts.

23. I need to (*transmit/apprehend*) a message to my cousin in Canada.

24. I (*assured/ensured/insured*) my mother that I would be home immediately after school.

25. Corinne suggested going out for pizza, which we all thought was a (*novel/novice*) idea.

26. My father is a (*connoisseur/interviewer*) of avocados; he knows more about avocados than anyone else I know.

27. Curtis told me his older brother is practically eight feet tall, but I know that's just (*hyperbole/literal*).

28. With her mastery of baton-twirling, Jane was (*uniquy/uniquely*) qualified to lead the parade.

29. You will get in a lot of trouble if you don't (*site/cite*) your sources on that assignment.

30. I was so (*sleepy/exhausted*) after working out that I could barely lift my arms.

MATCHING SYNONYMS

Match the word in the first column with its synonym in the second column.
Remember: Synonyms are words that have the same meaning.

31. chronically   **a.** slope

32. scintillating   **b.** guarantee

33. devise   **c.** habitually

34. enlightened   **d.** create

35. incline   **e.** worthless

36. rite   **f.** difficult

37. flammable   **g.** gorgeous

38. arduous   **h.** spirited

39. ensure   **i.** bitter

40. interrogate   **j.** insightful

41. useless   **k.** question

42. sublime   **l.** investigation

43. mischievous   **m.** sparkling

44. acidic   **n.** ritual

45. inquiry   **o.** inflammable

MATCHING ANTONYMS

Match the word in the first column with its antonym in the second column.
Remember: Antonyms are words that have opposite meanings.

46. sociable   **a.** hectic

47. clichéd   **b.** definite

48. erect   **c.** stand

49. precede   **d.** youthful

50. ambiguous   **e.** loud

51. tranquil   **f.** wild

52. thankful   **g.** meaningful

53. decrepit   **h.** wealthy

54. amigo   **i.** destroy

55. eloquent   **j.** fight

56. destitute   **k.** bashful

57. concede   **l.** enemy

58. recline   **m.** speechless

59. subtle   **n.** follow

60. domestic   **o.** thankless

ANSWERS

Sentence Completion

1. **b. multitalented.** You learned in Chapter 2 that the prefix *multi-* means "many." If Rodrigo can play several different instruments, then he has many talents, so the best choice is *multitalented*. Refresh your knowledge of prefixes in Chapter 2.

2. **c. diatribe.** As you learned in Chapter 6, a *diatribe* is an angry verbal attack. Although all of these words are synonyms, context clues tell you that the connotation of the correct word will be extremely negative. To learn more about context clues, revisit Chapter 6; to take another look at connotation, revisit Chapter 7.

3. **d. vary.** In Chapter 3, you learned that *varying* means "differing by degrees." The word *vary* is the verb form of the adjective *varying*. To learn more about adjectives, revisit Chapter 3.

4. **c. adequate.** Chapter 7 tells you how the best word choices will have the proper connotation. The sentence implies that the plumber's work was fine, but not outstanding; therefore, the best word is *adequate*. Refresh your knowledge of connotation by rereading Chapter 7.

5. **d. malfunction.** As you learned in the book, the prefix *mal-* means "bad, abnormal, evil, or wrong," and the word *function* means "job or role." Something that *malfunctions*, therefore, does a bad job, or does not work. To refresh your memory on suffixes and prefixes, revisit Chapter 2.

6. **stingy.** The connotation tells you that Renee has a very difficult time parting with money; the best word choice is *stingy*, meaning "cheap." Revisit connotations in Chapter 7.

7. **c. misinformed.** The prefix *mis-* means "bad, wrong, ill, opposite, or lack of." Context clues tell you that someone gave Kyle the wrong information, so the best choice is *misinformed*. For more about prefixes, reread Chapter 2; to refresh your knowledge of context clues, reread Chapter 6.

8. **a. incognito.** In Chapter 8, you learned that *incognito* is an Italian word meaning "in disguise." Read more about foreign words used in English by revisiting Chapter 8.

9. **d. simplistic.** Context and connotation clues tell you that the best choice is a word that means the opposite of "difficult." In Chapter 3, you

learned that *simplistic* means "in a simple or stupid manner"; therefore, *simplistic* is the best choice. To learn more about context, reread Chapter 6. Connotation can be studied by revisiting Chapter 7.

10. **c. parameters.** As you learned in the final chapter, *parameters* are limits. The context of this sentence should tell you that the teacher would like his students to stay with the limits of the assignment, or *parameters*. Learn more about very important words in Chapter 9.

11. **b. inaudible.** In Chapter 1, you learned that the word *audible* means "able to be heard." In Chapter 2, you learned that the prefix *in/il/im/ir* means "not." *Inaudible* is the best choice, meaning "not able to be heard." To refresh your memory on root words, take another look at Chapter 1. To revisit suffixes and prefixes, look at Chapter 2.

12. **c. debut.** As you learned in Chapter 8, *debut* is a French word that means "first performance." To learn more about foreign words used in English, take another look at Chapter 8.

13. **b. unenthusiastic.** You learned in Chapter 4 that *unenthusiastic* is a synonym for *unexcited*. Refresh your knowledge of synonyms by rereading that chapter.

14. **a. exceed.** In Chapter 1, you learned that the root *ced/ceed/cess* means "to go," and that *exceed* means "to go beyond." To refresh your memory on root words, take another look at that chapter.

15. **b. haphazardly.** In Chapter 6, you learned that *haphazard* means "careless." To turn the word *haphazard* into an adverb, add the suffix *-ly*. Revisit adverbs in Chapter 2; take another look at Chapter 6 to learn about using context to find the best word.

Choose the Right Word

16. **polluted.** In Chapter 1, you learned that to *dilute* is to make something thinner or to water it down, while to *pollute* is to make dirty. It is more likely that an oil spill would *pollute* the water, so this is the best choice. To learn more about word roots, reread Chapter 1.

17. **assent.** *Assent* and *ascent* are homonyms. *Assent* means "agreement," while an *ascent* is an upward climb. The best word here is *assent*. Revisit homonyms in Chapter 5.

18. **department.** As you learned in Chapter 9, a *department* is a small division within a corporation. Refresh your memory of important words about work in that chapter.

19. **unresponsive.** The word *responsive* means "responding to." To create an antonym of *responsive*, add the prefix *un-*. Refresh your understanding of prefixes by rereading Chapter 2.

20. **debatable.** In order to change the noun *debate* into an adjective, you should add the suffix *-able*. The suffix *-ify* is a verb ending. Revisit the differences between adjective endings and verb endings in Chapter 2.

21. **daunting.** In Chapter 3, you learned that the adjective *daunting* means "intimidating," while *dauntless* means "brave"; the best answer here is *daunting*. Read more about adjectives in that chapter.

22. **willpower.** In Chapter 7, you learned that *willpower* and *ambition* have different connotations. *Ambition* is drive, while *willpower* is the ability to avoid temptation. Learn more about connotation by revisiting that chapter.

23. **transmit.** In Chapter 4, you learned that *transmit* is a synonym for *send*. Revisit synonyms and antonyms in that chapter.

24. **assured.** As you learned in Chapter 5, *assured*, *ensured*, and *insured* are commonly confused words. The word choice that means "made someone feel confident" is *assured*. Revisit commonly confused words in that chapter.

25. **novel.** As you learned in Chapter 1, the root word *nov/neo/nou* means "new." A *novice* is a person who is new at something. The word *novice* refers to people, while the word *novel* means "a new, creative, or refreshing idea"; therefore, in this case, the best choice is *novel*. For more about word roots, revisit Chapter 1.

26. **connoisseur.** A *connoisseur* is an expert, as you learned in Chapter 8. Revisit that chapter to refresh your memory of foreign words.

27. **hyperbole.** *Hyperbole* is an important school word that was discussed in Chapter 9. It means "intentional exaggeration." Take another look at that chapter if you've forgotten the meaning of important school words.

28. **uniquely.** In Chapter 3, you learned that adverbs are words that modify adjectives. To turn the adjective *unique* into an adverb, add the suffix *-ly*. You can learn more about suffixes in Chapter 2, and you can learn more about adverbs by revisiting Chapter 3.

29. **cite.** *Cite*, *sight*, and *site* are homonyms. *Cite* means "refer to"; according to the sentence context, the best choice here is *cite*. Refresh your knowledge of homonyms in Chapter 5.

30. **exhausted.** Based on the sentence, you can tell that the best word will mean "extremely worn out." The word with the best connotation for this sentence is *exhausted*. Learn more about connotation in Chapter 7.

Matching Synonyms

31. (Chapter 1)	chronically	**c.** habitually
32. (Chapter 3)	scintillating	**m.** sparkling
33. (Chapter 4)	devise	**d.** create
34. (Chapter 7)	enlightened	**j.** insightful
35. (Chapter 1)	incline	**a.** slope
36. (Chapter 5)	rite	**n.** ritual
37. (Chapter 4)	flammable	**o.** inflammable
38. (Chapter 3)	arduous	**f.** difficult
39. (Chapter 5)	ensure	**b.** guarantee
40. (Chapter 1)	interrogate	**k.** question
41. (Chapter 4)	useless	**e.** worthless
42. (Chapter 6)	sublime	**g.** gorgeous
43. (Chapter 7)	mischievous	**h.** spirited
44. (Chapter 1)	acidic	**i.** bitter
45. (Chapter 9)	inquiry	**l.** investigation

Matching Antonyms

46. (Chapter 4)	sociable	**k.** bashful
47. (Chapter 9)	clichéd	**g.** meaningful
48. (Chapter 4)	erect	**i.** destroy
49. (Chapter 5)	precede	**n.** follow
50. (Chapter 9)	ambiguous	**b.** definite
51. (Chapter 1)	tranquil	**a.** hectic
52. (Chapter 4)	thankful	**o.** thankless
53. (Chapter 7)	decrepit	**d.** youthful
54. (Chapter 8)	amigo	**l.** enemy
55. (Chapter 3)	eloquent	**m.** speechless
56. (Chapter 7)	destitute	**h.** wealthy

57. (Chapter 6)   concede   **j.** fight

58. (Chapter 1)   recline   **c.** stand

59. (Chapter 3)   subtle   **e.** loud

60. (Chapter 4)   domestic   **f.** wild

Appendix A
Prefixes, Suffixes, and Word Roots

PREFIXES

The following table lists the most common English language prefixes, their meanings, and several examples of words with each prefix. Whenever possible, the examples include both common words that are already part of your everyday vocabulary and words from the lessons in this book.

PREFIX	MEANING	EXAMPLES
a-, an-	not, without	atypical, anarchy, amorphous
ab-, abs-	from, away, off	abnormal, abduct, abscond
ante-	prior to, in front of, before	antedate, antecedent, antebellum
ant-, anti-	opposite, opposing, against	antidote, antagonist, antipathy
bi-	two, twice	bisect, bilateral, bicameral
circum-	around, about, on all sides	circumference, circumnavigate, circumspect
co-, com-, con-	with, together, jointly	community, consensus cooperate
contra-	against, contrary, contrasting	contradict, contraindication
counter-	contrary, opposite or opposing; complementary	counterclockwise, countermeasure, counterpart
de-	do the opposite or reverse of; remove from, reduce	deactivate, dethrone, detract

PREFIX	MEANING	EXAMPLES
dis-	away from, apart, reversal, not	disperse, dismiss, disinterested
duo-	two	duo, duet, duality
ex-	out, out of, away from	expel, exclaim, exorbitant
in- (*also* il-, im-, ir-)	in, into, within	induct, impart, inculcate
in- (*also* il-, im-, ir-)	not	invariable, incessant, illicit, inept, impervious
inter-	between, among, within	intervene, interact, intermittent
intra-	within, during	intramural, intravenous
intro-	in, into, within	introvert, introduction
mal-	bad, abnormal, evil, wrong	malfunction, malpractice, malign
mis-	bad, wrong, ill; opposite; lack of	misspell, miscreant, misanthrope
mono-	one, single, alone	monologue, monogamy, monocle
multi-	many, multiple	multiple, multimillionaire, multifarious
neo-	new, recent, a new form of	neologism, neonatal, neophyte
non-	not	nonconformist, nonentity, nonchalant
over-	exceeding, surpassing, excessive	overabundance, overstimulate
poly-	many, much	polyester, polytechnic, polyglot
post-	after, subsequent, later (than), behind	postpone, postpartum, postoperative
pre-	before	precaution, precede, presage
pro-	(a) earlier, before, prior to; in front of; (b) for, supporting, in behalf of; (c) forward, projecting	proceed, proclivity, profess
pseudo-	false, fake	pseudonym, pseudoscience
re-	back, again	recall, reconcile, rescind
semi-	half, partly, incomplete	semiannual, semiconscious
sub-	under, beneath, below	subconscious, subdue, subjugate
super-	above, over, exceeding	superhero, superficial, supercilious
trans-	across, beyond, through	transmit, translate, translucent
tri-	three, thrice	triangle, tricycle, triumvirate
un-	not	unable, uninterested, unorthodox
uni-	one	unite, uniform, unilateral

SUFFIXES

The following table lists the most common English language suffixes, their meanings, and several examples of words with each suffix. Whenever possible, the examples include both common words that are already part of your everyday vocabulary and words from the lessons in this book.

NOUN ENDINGS

SUFFIX	MEANING	EXAMPLES
-age	(a) action or process (b) house or place of (c) state, rank	drainage, orphanage, marriage
-al	action or process	rehearsal, disposal, reversal
-an, -ian	of or relating to; a person specializing in	guardian, pediatrician, historian
-ance, -ence	action or process; state of	adolescence, benevolence, renaissance
-ancy, -ency	quality or state	agency, vacancy, latency
-ant, -ent	one that performs, promotes, or causes an action; being in a specified state or condition	disinfectant, dissident, miscreant
-ary	thing belonging to or connected with	adversary, dignitary, library
-cide	killer, killing	suicide, pesticide, homicide
-cy	action or practice; state or quality of	democracy, legitimacy, supremacy
-er, -or	one that is, does, or performs	builder, foreigner, sensor
-ion, -tion	act or process; state or condition	attraction, persecution, denunciation
-ism	act, practice, or process; state or doctrine of	criticism, anachronism, imperialism
-ist	one who (performs, makes, produces, believes, etc.)	anarchist, feminist, imperialist
-ity	quality, state, or degree	clarity, amity, veracity
-ment	action or process; result, object, means, or agent of an action or process	entertainment, embankment, amazement
-ness	state, condition, quality, or degree	happiness, readiness, goodness
-ology	doctrine, theory, or science; oral or written expression	biology, theology, eulogy
-or	condition, activity	candor, valor, succor
-sis	process or action	diagnosis, dialysis, metamorphosis
-ure	act or process; office or function	exposure, legislature, censure
-y	state, condition, quality; activity or place of business	laundry, empathy, anarchy

ADJECTIVE ENDINGS

SUFFIX	MEANING	EXAMPLES
-able, -ible	capable or worthy of; tending or liable to	flammable, culpable, inscrutable
-al, -ial, -ical	having the quality of; of, relating to, or characterized by	educational, peripheral, ephemeral
-an, -ian	one who is or does; related to, characteristic of	human, American, agrarian
-ant, -ent	performing (a specific action) or being (in a specified condition)	important, incessant, preeminent
-ful	full of; having the qualities of; tending or liable to	helpful, peaceful, wistful
-ic	pertaining or relating to; having the quality of	fantastic, chronic, archaic
-ile	tending to or capable of	fragile, futile, servile
-ish	having the quality of	Swedish, bookish, squeamish
-ive	performing or tending toward (an action); having the nature of	sensitive, cooperative, pensive
-less	without, lacking; unable to act or be acted on (in a specified way)	endless, fearless, listless
-ous, -ose,	full of, having the qualities of, relating to	adventurous, glorious, egregious
-y	characterized by, full of; tending or inclined to	sleepy, cursory, desultory

VERB ENDINGS

SUFFIX	MEANING	EXAMPLES
-ate	to make, to cause to be or become	violate, tolerate, exacerbate, emanate
-en	to cause to be or have; to come to be or have	quicken, lengthen, frighten
-ify, -fy	to make, form into	beautify, electrify, rectify
-ize	to cause to be or become; to bring about	colonize, plagiarize, synchronize

WORD ROOTS

The following table lists the most common word roots, their meanings, and several examples of words with those roots. Whenever possible, the examples include both common words that are already part of your everyday vocabulary and words from the chapters in this book.

There are more than 150 roots here, but don't be intimidated by the length of this list. Break it down into manageable chunks of 10–20 roots and memorize them section by section. Remember that you use words with these roots every day.

ROOT	MEANING	EXAMPLES
ac, acr	sharp, bitter	acid, acute, acrimonious
act, ag	to do, to drive, to force, to lead	agent, enact, agitate
ad, al	to, toward, near	adjacent, adhere, allure
al, ali, alter	other, another	alternative, alias, alien
am	love	amiable, amity, enamor
amb	to go, to walk	ambulatory, preamble, ambush
amb, amph	both, more than one, around	ambiguous, ambivalent, amphitheater
anim	life, mind, soul, spirit	unanimous, animosity, equanimity
annui, ennui	year	annual, anniversary, perennial
anthro, andr	man, human	anthropology, android, misanthrope
apo	away	apology, apocalypse, apotheosis
apt, ept	skill, fitness, ability	adapt, adept, inept
arch, archi, archy	chief, principal, ruler	hierarchy, monarchy, anarchy
auto	self	automatic, autonomy, automaton
be	to be, to have a certain quality	befriend, bemoan, belittle
bel, bell	war	rebel, belligerent, antebellum
ben, bon	good	benefit, benevolent, bonus
cad, cid	to fall, to happen by chance	accident, coincidence, cascade
cant, cent, chant	to sing	chant, enchant, recant
cap, capit, cipit	head, headlong	capital, principal, capitulate
cap, cip, cept	to take, to get	capture, intercept, emancipate
card, cord, cour	heart	encourage, cardiac, discord
carn	flesh	carnivore, reincarnation, carnage
cast, chast	cut	caste, chastise, castigate
ced, ceed, cess	to go, to yield, to stop	exceed, concede, incessant
centr	center	central, concentric, eccentric
cern, cert, cret, crim, crit	to separate, to judge, to distinguish, to decide	ascertain, critique, discern
chron	time	chronic, chronology, synchronize
cis	to cut	scissors, precise, incisive
cla, clo, clu	shut, close	closet, enclose, preclude
claim, clam	to shout, to cry out	exclaim, proclaim, clamor
cli, clin	to lean toward, bend	decline, recline, proclivity
cour, cur	running, a course	recur, incursion, cursory
crat, cracy	to govern	democracy, autocracy, bureaucracy
cre, cresc, cret	to grow	creation, increase, increment
cred	to believe, to trust	incredible, credit, incredulous
cryp	hidden	crypt, cryptic, cryptography
cub, cumb	to lie down	succumb, incubate, incumbent
culp	blame	culprit, culpable, exculpate

ROOT	MEANING	EXAMPLES
dac, doc	to teach	doctor, indoctrinate, docile
dem	people	democracy, epidemic, pandemic
di, dia	apart, through	dialogue, diatribe, dichotomy
dic, dict, dit	to say, to tell, to use words	predict, dictionary, indict
dign	worth	dignity, indignant, disdain
dog, dox	opinion	dogma, orthodox, paradox
dol	suffer, pain	condolence, indolence, dolorous
don, dot, dow	to give	donate, endow
dub	doubt	dubious, indubitable, dubiety
duc, duct	to lead	conduct, induct, conducive
dur	hard	endure, durable, obdurate
dys	faulty, abnormal	dysfunctional, dystopia, dyslexia
epi	upon	epidemic, epigram, epigraph
equ	equal, even	equation, equanimity, equivocate
err	to wander	err, error, erratic
esce	becoming	adolescent, coalesce, acquiesce
eu	good, well	euphoria, eulogy, euthanasia
fab, fam	speak	fable, famous, affable
fac, fic, fig, fait, feit, fy	to do, to make	fiction, factory, feign
fer	to bring, to carry, to bear	offer, transfer, proliferate
ferv	to boil, to bubble	fervor, fervid, effervescent
fid	faith, trust	confide, fidelity, infidel
fin	end	final, finite, affinity
flag, flam	to burn	flame, flammable, inflammatory
flect, flex	to bend	deflect, reflect, flexible
flu, flux	to flow	fluid, fluctuation, superfluous
fore	before	foresight, forestall, forebear
fort	chance	fortune, fortunate, fortuitous
fra, frac, frag, fring	to break	fracture, fraction, infringe
fus	to pour	confuse, infusion, diffuse
gen	birth, creation, race, kind	generous, genetics, homogenous
gn, gno	to know	ignore, recognize, incognito
grad, gress	to step	progress, aggressive, digress
grat	pleasing	grateful, gratitude, ingratiate
her, hes	to stick	cohere, adherent, inherent
hetero	different, other	heterosexual, heterogeneous, heterodox
(h)om	same	homogeneous, homonym, anomaly
hyper	over, excessive	hyperactive, hyperextend, hyperbole

ROOT	MEANING	EXAMPLES
id	one's own	idiom, idiosyncrasy, ideology
ject	to throw, to throw down	eject, dejected, conjecture
join, junct	to meet, to join	joint, junction, juxtapose
jur	to swear	jury, perjury, abjure
lect, leg	to select, to choose	election, select, eclectic
lev	lift, light, rise	elevator, lever, alleviate
loc, log, loqu	word, speech	dialogue, eloquent, loquacious
luc, lum, lus	light	illustrate, lucid, luminous
lud, lus	to play	illusion, elude, allude
lug, lut, luv	to wash	lavatory, dilute, deluge
mag, maj, max	big	magnify, magnitude, magnanimous
man	hand	manual, manufacture, manifest
min	small	minute, diminish, minutiae
min	to project, to hang over	prominent, imminent, preeminent
mis, mit	to send	transmit, remit, intermittent
mon, monit	to warn	monitor, admonish, remonstrate
morph	shape	amorphous, metamorphosis, anthropomorphic
mort	death	immortal, morbid, moratorium
mut	change	mutate, immutable, permutation
nam, nom, noun, nown, nym	rule, order	economy, taxonomy, autonomy
nat, nas, nai	to be born	native, nascent, renaissance
nec, nic, noc, nox	harm, death	innocent, noxious, innocuous
nom, nym, noun, nown	name	nominate, homonym, nominal
nounc, nunc	to announce	announce, pronounce, denounce
nov, neo, nou	new	novice, novel, neophyte
ob, oc, of, op	toward, to, against, completely, over	object, obstruct, obsequious
omni	all	omnipresent, omnipotent, omniscient
pac, peas	peace	pacify, appease, pacifier
pan	all, everyone	panorama, pandemic, panacea
par	equal	par, disparate, parity
para	next to, beside	parallel, paragon, paradox
pas, pat, path	feeling, suffering, disease	passionate, antipathy, apathetic
pau, po, pov, pu	few, little, poor	poverty, pauper, impoverish
ped	child, education	pediatrician, encyclopedia, pedantic
ped, pod	foot	pedestrian, expedite, impede
pen, pun	to pay, to compensate	penalty, punishment, penance
pend, pens	to hang, to weigh, to pay	depend, compensate, pensive

ROOT	MEANING	EXAMPLES
per	completely, wrong	perplex, permeate, pervade
peri	around	perimeter, peripheral, peripatetic
pet, pit	to go, to seek, to strive	compete, petition, impetuous
phil	love	philosophy, philanthropy, bibliophile
phone	sound	telephone, homophone, cacophony
plac	to please	placid, placebo, complacent
ple	to fill	complete, deplete, plethora
plex, plic, ply	to fold, to twist, to tangle, to bend	complex, comply, implicit
pon, pos, pound	to put, to place	expose, component, juxtapose
port	to carry	import, portable, importune
prehend, prise	to take, to get, to seize	surprise, apprehend, reprisal
pro	much, for, a lot	proliferate, profuse, proselytize
prob	to prove, to test	probe, probation, reprobate
pug	to fight	repugnant, pugnacious, impugn
punc, pung, poign	to point, to prick	point, puncture, punctilious
que, quis	to seek	inquisitive, conquest, query
qui	quiet	quiet, tranquil, acquiesce
rid, ris	to laugh	riddle, ridiculous, derision
rog	to ask	interrogate, surrogate, abrogate
sacr, sanct, secr	sacred	sacred, sacrament, sanction
sal, sil, sault, sult	to leap, to jump	assault, insolent, desultory
sci	to know	conscious, science, omniscient
scribe, scrip	to write	scribble, prescribe, circumscribe
se	apart	separate, segregate, seditious
sec, sequ	to follow	consequence, sequel, obsequious
sed, sess, sid	to sit, to be still, to plan, to plot	subside, assiduous, dissident
sens, sent	to feel, to be aware	sense, sentiment, dissent
sol	to loosen, to free	dissolve, resolution, dissolution
spec, spic, spit	to look, to see	perspective, speculation, circumspect
sta, sti	to stand, to be in place	static, obstinate, steadfast
sua	smooth	suave, persuade, dissuade
tac, tic	to be silent	tacit, reticent, taciturn
tain, ten, tent, tin	to hold	detain, sustain, tenacious
tend, tens, tent, tenu	to stretch, to thin	extend, tension, tenuous
theo	god	atheist, theology, apotheosis
tract	to drag, to pull, to draw	attract, detract, tractable
us, ut	to use	abuse, utility, usurp
ven, vent	to come, to move toward	convene, venture, intervene

ROOT	MEANING	EXAMPLES
ver	truth	verdict, verisimilitude, veritable
vers, vert	to turn	revert, aversion, versatile
vi	life	vivid, vigorous, vicarious
vid, vis	to see	evident, survey, visionary
voc, vok	to call	vocal, advocate, equivocate
vol	to wish	volunteer, volition, benevolence

Appendix B
Common Acronyms and Abbreviations

ABBREVIATIONS

The following is a list of common abbreviations you may come across in reading, separated into categories.

Grammar

adj.	adjective
adv.	adverb
colloq.	colloquially; indicates a slang term
conj.	conjunction
encycl.	encyclopedia
Eng.	English
indef.	indefinite
int.	interjection
int.	interrogative
intr.	intransitive
irreg.	irregular
n.	noun
obj.	object
pl.	plural
pref.	prefix
prep.	preposition
pronunc.	pronunciation

subj.	subject
suff.	suffix
syll.	syllable
wd.	word

Sayings and Useful Terms

btw.	between
c	circa; at or around the time of (c 1826, for example)
e.g.	*exempli gratia*: Latin for "for example"
esp.	especially
et al.	*et alia*: Latin for "and others"
etc.	*et cetera*: Latin for "and so on"
i.e.	*id est*: Latin for "that is"
rev.	revised
w/o	without

Time

A.D.	*anno domini*: used to refer to the years 1–the present
A.M.	*ante meridiem*; the hours between midnight and 11:59 in the morning
Apr.	April
Aug.	August
B.C.	Before Christ; the time before A.D.
BCE	Before Common Era; is often used in place of B.C.
c.	century
CE	Common Era; is often used in place of A.D.
Dec.	December
Feb.	February
hrs.	hours
Jan.	January
Jul.	July
Jun.	June
Mar.	March
min.	minute
Nov.	November
Oct.	October
P.M.	post meridiem; the hours between noon and 11:59 at night

sec.	seconds
Sept.	September

Business

assoc.	associated
co.	company
corp.	corporation
inst.	institute
ltd.	limited
re.	regarding

Place

ave.	avenue
ct.	court
dr.	drive
ln.	lane
rd.	road
st.	street

Units of Measurement

c.	cup
fl. oz.	fluid ounce
ft.	feet
g	gram
in.	inches
kg	kilogram
km	kilometer
L	liter
lb.	pound
m	meter
mi.	mile
ml	milliliter
oz.	ounce
tbsp.	tablespoon
tsp.	teaspoon

People

Dr.	doctor
MD	medical doctor
PhD	doctorate of philosophy
pres.	president
prof.	professor
RN	registered nurse
VP	vice president

ACRONYMS

Acronyms are words that are created by taking the first letter of each word in a phrase or proper name. Here are common acronyms in the English language.

AIDS	acquired immune deficiency syndrome
AWOL	absent without leave
BCC	blind carbon copy
BTW	by the way
CC	carbon copy
CD-ROM	compact disc read-only memory
CEO	chief executive officer
CIA	Central Intelligence Agency
CPU	central processing unit
DJ	disc jockey
DNA	deoxyribonucleic acid
DVD	digital video disc
ER	emergency room
FAA	Federal Aviation Administration
FBI	Federal Bureau of Investigation
FYI	for your information
IQ	intelligence quotient
IRS	Internal Revenue Service
LASER	light amplificiation by stimulated emission of radiation
MBA	master of business administration
MC	master of ceremonies

MIA	missing in action
NASA	National Aeronautics and Space Administration
NATO	North Atlantic Treaty Organization
POW	prisoner of war
PTA	Parent Teacher Association
SAT	Scholastic Assessment Test
SCUBA	self-contained underwater breathing apparatus
TBA	to be announced
TBD	to be determined
TM	trademark
UFO	unidentified flying object
USA	United States of America

Notes